Happy Christ

from

975.

Back to the Mark

BACK TO

As told to IAN BRAYSHAW

DENNIS LILLEE

THE MARK

STANLEY PAUL London

STANLEY PAUL & CO. LTD
3 Fitzroy Square, London W1

AN IMPRINT OF THE HUTCHINSON GROUP

London Melbourne Sydney Auckland
Wellington Johannesburg Cape Town
and agencies throughout the world

First published 1974

This book has been set in Intertype Baskerville
by Meredith Trade Lino, Melbourne
Printed by The Griffin Press Adelaide

ISBN 009 123130 2

Foreword by Richie Benaud

Test cricketers come and go; batsmen abound and slow bowlers, either left or right hand, find their way into every international team. So too do medium pacers. But undoubtedly the most exciting sight of all is that of a great batsman in action or a great fast bowler tearing in past the umpire.

McDonald and Gregory, Lindwall and Miller — they were the best known fast bowling *pairs* known to Australian cricket. Others of less pace were fine bowlers, like Alan Davidson, arguably the greatest left hand pace bowler, and Graham McKenzie, another of stature. The latter pair suffered from the same disability that Dennis Lillee encountered — the lack of a really fast bowler at the other end over a number of years.

Dennis came into Test cricket in the 1970-71 series against England in Australia, an event that is covered more than adequately in this book. What is not generally known though is that circumstances forced the Australian selectors to choose him a little earlier than they originally intended.

There was no doubt he was splendid raw material — a little too raw at the time, with his sprawling delivery stride and unbalanced action.

By the time the Rest of the World team came to Australia the following season, he had a lot of that sorted out and, when Ian Chappell's team reached England in 1972, Dennis was very much the trump card.

Since that triumph life hasn't been all that easy for the back trouble that beset him in May 1972 returned and, as I write this, he is beginning the long, hard road back to complete *bowling* fitness. I stress the distinction, for it is quite an easy thing to be fully fit yet not be completely fit to bowl fast. If he manages to have it all come right by December then the sight of Lillee and Rod Marsh crouching some 75 yards away will once again thrill spectators and T.V. watchers.

A medium pacer taking a long run is a bore — a really fast bowler is the only one who needs that and I must confess to excitement when Lindwall, Tyson, Statham, Trueman, Hall and Lillee turned as a prelude to pounding in at the batsman.

If he is fit enough to do it again in this 1974-75 season in Australia, then Australia's chances of regaining the Ashes are immeasurably improved but, that apart, he has plenty of interesting points to make in his story so far.

Dennis makes no secret of the fact that he prefers the comforts of home life to touring overseas and he will always go for an occasional beer and a hearty steak rather than a Chateau Latour and Pheasant a la Souvaroff. I've never known, in any case, a good fast bowler who trained on pheasant!

If, as I believe, Australia's chances are improved with his availability in 1974-75, so too are the spectators' chances of seeing exciting cricket. More power to him — I hope his comeback and his book hit the high peaks of success.

Richie Benaud

Illustrations

Acknowledgements

Many people have helped to make this book possible. I would particularly like to thank the following for their assistance, encouragement, patience and understanding: Singapore Airlines; Ian Brayshaw and his wife Joan; Richie Benaud; John Inverarity; Peter Waltham; WA Newpapers Ltd (particularly Norman Taylor and Syd Downer); Leon Larkin of Travel-Time International; WA Cricket Association; and Peter Taylor of the Hutchinson Group, Australia.

Finally, I wish to acknowledge the great debt I owe to my wife, Helen, not only for her patience while this book was being written, but for all the support she gave me when I needed it most.

Dennis Lillee

1

A warm sun was picking gaps in a generous cloud cover over the Sydney Cricket Ground and a gentle breeze moved scraps of paper on The Hill. It was Wednesday, 12 January 1972, and there was a goodish crowd watching the second last day of the fourth international against Gary Sobers' Rest of the World team. Australia had a stranglehold on the game and the series was tied at 1-1. We were more than 500 runs ahead with a day and a half to play. The little Indian, Sunil Gavaskar, and the burly South African, Hylton Ackerman, were in the throes of making a solid opening for the tourists.

But the series, promoted by a big Australian newspaper chain when the proposed tour of Australia by South Africa fell through, was beginning to drag for me. I had been away from home for over a month, and had missed having Christmas with my wife, Helen. It was my seventh game in eight weeks, and it was only a few days since I had wheeled down 30 overs on the unrelenting turf of the Melbourne Cricket Ground, to the broad, almost smiling bat of Sobers in his mammoth innings of 254. My mind was starting to drift ahead to possible selection in the Australian team for the tour of England in a couple of months time. I was going to have to bowl many, many overs there, it seemed. Then I was thinking about Helen, who I would see again in two days time. But, there was another day of this match to play, and there was a game to be won.

The wicket, which had started out so much in favour of the fast bowlers, now was a featherbed. The Australian second innings had produced 546, 119 to Ian Chappell and 197 not out to his brother Greg, and now it seemed the Rest of the World batsmen would take some shifting. I was feeling pretty tired and I must admit I was bowling at not much above medium pace. Then Ian Chappell approached me before I started my seventh over of the innings. 'Look here,' he said, 'if I want somebody to bowl spinners, I'll ask Terry Jenner to have a go.' He said it in a joking manner, but at the same time he was giving me a pretty broad hint that I should liven things up a bit. That rankled me a bit, in a way I suppose I was insulted. Anyway, as I stalked back to the top of my mark under the shadow of the giant M. A. Noble stand at the northern end of the ground I was determined to show Ian Chappell that I *could* bowl fast.

I took a deep breath and ran the 30-yard approach at full speed. The ball flew down at Gavaskar yards faster than my previous deliveries, but there was no satisfaction for me. At the end of my follow-through I was wracked with pain stabbing into my back somewhere near the base of my spine.

For some seconds I stood there clutching my back and wondering what had happened to me. The next thing I knew Chappell was by my side. I told him what had happened. 'Try to finish the over,' he said. I went back and went through all the motions of bowling, but there was nothing there. I couldn't put any 'back' into it at all. The very best I could do was make my arm flow through something like its normal arc. But what came out was pitiful. It might as well have been Terry Jenner, except that they weren't turning enough. I staggered through the rest of the over, then immediately left the field, still in considerable pain.

The physiotherapist at the Sydney Cricket Ground, Dave McErlane, got me on the rub-down table and gave my back a thorough inspection. He was clearly concerned about things, because he immediately called the cricket ground doctor, Brian Corrigan. He also examined me thoroughly and gave the first diagnosis: 'It's probably muscular trouble.' At that stage I had no idea of the implications of it all. I had never had a lasting injury before and I was sure that with maybe a few days rest and treatment I'd be back on the road again soon. I rang Helen from the team motel that night as I knew she would have heard that I'd left the field and not returned and naturally would be worried as to the extent of the injury. There was an anxious voice at the other end of the line, but I reassured her. 'Don't worry, it's only a muscular injury. It's just a matter of resting and I'll be all right.'

Looking for reasons why my back should have given in, I can only point to the stiff programme I had faced leading up to that fateful day at the SCG. In the 1970-71 season I had bowled a lot of overs for Western Australia, played in the last two Tests against Ray Illingworth's team and immediately left the country to take a professional appointment with the Lancashire League club, Haslingden. I had a fairly hectic season in the League, and then almost sprinted home to pick up with the new Australian season. There was virtually no break again as I hurried through training sessions that were aimed at holding me up for the remainder of the season. I was reasonably happy with my condition when the first-class season got under way late in October. Then, from 20 November through to 12 January I had only one week off. That was the game between Western Australia and the Rest of the World, in Perth, when the State selectors gave me a spell so they could try out some other local fast bowlers. Perhaps the 'back-breaker' was the second innings of the Melbourne international when I bowled those 30 overs. Anyway, in those six games leading up to the Sydney game I had sent down 166.2 overs in first-class games (plus eight in an unscheduled one-day game against the tourists when the Perth international finished early) for 44 wickets at a cost of 646 runs. That might not sound much, but on the hard Australian wickets and in the heat of an Australian summer — and bowling every ball flat out — it was pretty tough going. Then I bowled 19 overs in the first innings of the Sydney game, so I guess my back was just making its own kind of protest.

That was the end of that game for me. I was suffering so much that I couldn't even act as the team's 12th man. I was in pain even walking about. Any movement provoked pain, but there was a sharp reaction whenever I made a sideways turn or stretched my legs a bit. That night I had trouble finding a comfortable position in bed, and could only sleep by lying flat on my back. Getting dressed was an act all of its own. I had to sit gingerly on the edge of my bed and slowly ease myself into my clothes from that position. I had to edge my feet carefully into each shoe and then ask my roommate to do up my laces for me. I flew home straight away.

The first part of my rest period was a trip to Yanchep, a holiday resort about 50 miles north of Perth, which was arranged by a Perth television channel. We called at the studios on our way and had a long interview where my back injury and plans were discussed at length. Then I tried to put the matter out of my mind for a few relaxing days. But that wasn't always possible as I found when we went for a row in a dinghy on the lake at Yanchep. I rowed about 50 yards from the shore, drifting fairly easily with the wind, but when I tried to put in another stroke with the oars I collapsed in a heap of pain in the bottom of the dinghy. Helen had to take over the oars and we really struggled to make shore against the wind and tide. During our stay there I was able to watch my mate Bob Massie in action on the television taking three wickets in a one-day game against the Rest of the World in Melbourne. I had withdrawn from that game and the one scheduled for Sydney the day before.

Back in Perth a few days later I was examined by an orthopaedic surgeon, who had received instructions from Brian Corrigan to give me continued treatment for muscular trouble.

Brian had also ordered X-rays to be taken of my back, but they revealed nothing. I probably put the doctors off in their investigations because I maintained that I was suffering pain in an area about four inches away from the part of my spine where stress fractures had actually begun to appear. It is something called referred pain.

Still I wasn't particularly worried about things, even though the tour of England was only a couple of months away and I was determined to be in the team and fit to do my best.

The doctor in Perth gave me a series of stretching exercises to ease the muscular pain. I went to see him daily for a week or so and gradually things improved, probably because I was off training and was resting the injured area. Nearly a fortnight after I had broken down in Sydney I was given the all-clear by the doctor to resume jogging and light exercise, and a week later I was allowed to return to the nets.

I bowled some medium-pacers and all seemed well. It was about a week before WA's next Sheffield Shield game, against New South Wales in Perth, and I badly wanted to play because we were hot on the trail of a third Shield title for our State. But I suffered a setback when I contracted influenza and was in bed for three days. I was still determined to play, so it was out of bed and into the nets to prove my fitness for the game. I bowled a few overs and, although feeling a bit weak, built up enough pace to pass the test. On reflection I guess I couldn't have done anything more inane that get out of a sickbed, such a short time after I'd broken down, to play a tough four-day game. But when you are young and enthusiastic you'll try anything once. I thought I was fit, but I wasn't.

It was an extremely easy-paced wicket at the WACA Ground and NSW ambled along to 524 before declaring with seven wickets down. Alan Turner, the opener, had collected 127 and Doug Walters was not out on 163. My pace just wasn't there and I ended up sore and sorry for myself with no wicket for 119 from 19 rather innocuous overs.

I was really flattened by that game and decided to give it away and rest up for the coming tour of England. I went back to the orthopaedic surgeon, who agreed and prescribed more treatment from a physiotherapist, checking on my progress himself every couple of days. That went on for a couple of weeks, then came the cruncher — I had to pass a fitness test to go to England. The other five West Australians, John Inverarity, Rod Marsh, Ross Edwards, Graeme Watson and Bob Massie, were holding their own practice sessions at the WACA Ground to keep in nick for the tour.

So one afternoon I joined them and had my own fitness test, which consisted of bowling a few overs at just above medium pace. I reported to the cricket association doctor, who put me through some exercises in his surgery and then put a tick against my name for the tour. It was such a short time after I had broken down in Sydney, and only a few weeks since I had staggered through the Shield game, then missing the latter part of the season, that perhaps it was a mistake to leave Australia with Ian Chappell's team.

2

There are a lot of things in life which I have to be thankful for, not least of which is my particularly happy childhood. I was born in Perth on 18 July 1949 and at that time my mother was only 19 and my father 22. I have always been grateful for having such young parents because it made it so much easier for us all to get on well together. In fact, with my younger brother and sister, all five of us virtually grew up together, and we've certainly not been troubled with a generation gap! Dad was always young and active enough to keep pace with the three of us as we raced through our early days, and he's still fit enough to have a social game with Perth Cricket Club every summer and not really notice his age.

Our family nearly always did things together as a unit, perhaps watching one of us play sport or going on a family picnic or whatever. Sunday was usually a family day and we'd often make the trip down to Jarrahdale, a timber town about thirty-five miles south of Perth where Dad's family lived. My mother's family lived much closer and we were able to visit them often during the week.

I was lucky to have a brother, Trevor, only 18 months younger than me and we had so much in common that we were inseparable mates. From an early age Trevor was a very clever sportsman and so we were able to play a lot of games together. In fact there was often a struggle for supremacy even then, despite the age difference. Our sister, Carmen, almost four years younger, also showed aptitude towards sports and often joined in games with the two of us.

Being an athlete has been a great part of my life, but it didn't come naturally to me. As a youngster I had great difficulty staying on my feet. I was so inclined to collapse at the ankles and fall over that my parents finally bought special boots to support my ankles and help me walk properly. Later, when I tried to join my friends in a run round, it was not at all uncommon for me to simply fall over as I ran. This was embarrassing, especially as it persisted into my early school days and I had developed a funny sort of gait because of lack of confidence in my step. But I determined to throw this thing off and get rid of those horrible ankle-high boots I was still wearing, so I taught myself a new style of walking and running so that I could stand upright with the best of my mates.

We were always very active children and my mother must have been relieved when I started school at the Belmay Primary School not far from our home in Belmont. I was never more than an average student and must admit I was always more interested in the final bell each day so I could get out and play games with my friends. It was at Belmay that I met my first sporting influence outside my family. He was a schoolteacher called Ken Watters, an unlikely looking sportsman with a light build and red hair, but with the ability to impart a fundamental knowledge of games and a will to win. In those days I was just as keen on swimming and football as I was on cricket, but my enthusiasm for swimming, at which I had advanced to a fair standard and captaincy of the Primary School team in my final year, dropped off in my early teens. My father had been something of a footballer in his day, and my environment was far more attuned to football than cricket. It was pure chance that I began to develop as a cricketer, but fortunately for Trevor and me Dad became quite keen on the game and it was he who guided us along the path as best he could when we were both very young. His father was very keen on cricket and used to keep Trevor and me enthralled for hours talking about the game, but he could never participate with us because he was confined to bed for many years before he died in 1970. Mum's father, on the other hand, was and still is very active and he not only gave us similar instruction but was also able to get down to the game with us as well.

As far back as I can remember we had a cricket bat and ball of sorts and a game going in the backyard of our house, or somewhere in the neighbourhood. Dad was a truck driver and often didn't get home till quite late in summer evenings, but there was always enough daylight left to squeeze in a game before he sat down to tea. I can remember the scramble to get the game set up as soon as we heard Dad arriving home. We always just 'happened' to be playing cricket when Dad came into sight around the side of the house. And, no matter how weary he was from the day's work, Dad would always oblige us, our eyes asking all sorts of questions. The older he gets, the more proficient Dad becomes at cricket, but in those days he really used to struggle. But he could bowl some pretty big breaks on the soft, spongy surface of the back lawn and the mixture he sent down with our rubber composition ball always kept us on our toes. We were at our wits ends to defend our wickets at times and I think that's where my brother, who became a regular first-grade club batsman at an early age, and I learned the rudiments of batting.

That's how it all started, and it was Dad's interest that kept us at it when perhaps we might have fallen by the wayside. Quite naturally, as we grew older our games became far more sophisticated. We graduated from the back lawn to the front lawn of our house, to any other lawn that offered itself to our particular brand of destruction, or to a park that wasn't too far away. Our knock-up games became 'Test' matches on the highest plane. We would roll the grass, mow it close and generally nurture a strip that would do any suburban 'Test' match proud. Then the neighbourhood would line up for 'selection', teams would be appointed, names of the stars of the day and their country adopted, the toss (flats or rounds with the cricket bat) effected and play begun. We had all the trimmings: umpires, scoreboards and even the odd female spectator. They were legendary encounters, hammer and tongs till darkness or a mother's call to tea. We longed for weekends, for then we could play a full 'Test' series if we were lucky. Imaginations ran wild as 'Davidson', 'Benaud' and 'Harvey' took the field against 'Dexter', 'Trueman' and 'May' at our own 'Lord's' ground. Perhaps the best strip we had in those early days was in the backyard of a neighbouring house where our cricket friend, Chris McLeod, lived. The wicket was bare of grass, rolled out hard with all the loose sand swept away and we used old tennis balls which didn't bounce too much. We were able to bowl as fast or slow as we liked, or were able to, and this was where I started my career as a fast bowler. It was a real test in every sense of the word. The bowler's run-up was a cramped five paces — a little shorter than my approach to the wicket in more recent years! The delivery point got so scoured out by constant use that we finally dug it out a little more and laid an old soft mattress there to give the bowlers a foothold. It was a foothold, but a very treacherous one, because if you tended to topple a bit you would soon find yourself on your back. It slowed us down a little, but I think that mattress taught me a few lessons about the importance of being upright at the delivery point. I certainly didn't fancy the chortles of delight from 'Dexter' and 'Cowdrey' each time I tumbled over, so balance became important even at that early stage.

In those days I batted as much and as earnestly as I bowled. In all my early competitive cricket I was either an opening batsman or No. 3, never lower. And the only time I haven't opened the bowling (with the wind) for my side was one season for Western Australia, when Graham McKenzie had precedence, and with the Perth Cricket Club in the 1973-4 season when I was gingerly making a comeback to bowling. I always had a long run-up, when the arena permitted, and my friends used to rib me about that, saying 'look out, here comes Wes Hall!'.

I must admit that big Wes had an enormous influence on me. I used to go into raptures watching him in action. His long, awesome run-up, the explosive delivery and the lightning-fast balls were my ideals. To be as good and fast as Wes Hall was a goal that spurred me on and on. Indeed, my mates weren't far off the mark with their 'here comes Wes' jibes, because in my childlike ways I did imagine myself to be the giant West Indian sending 'em down. One day my brother and I jumped over the back fence at the WA Cricket Association Ground in Perth just to see Wes in full flight. We just *had* to get into the members' enclosure, just to be near the big fellow, just to let a bit of his magic rub off. Our luck was in . . . Wes was out in front of the players' pavilion, sitting in the middle of a gang of gawkers like ourselves. We clamoured around him for what seemed like eternity, firing questions like a machine-gun and Wes never tired of answering our questions, most of which must have been absolutely stupid. He seemed to love it and that personal touch made an everlasting impression on me. I floated home that night and the next time I bowled at the lads it was an inspired Dennis Lillee who let a few go at surprising pace.

Though Wes was my main inspiration, of course Graham McKenzie, being a West Australian, had a special bearing on me. When Wes was far away I always had Garth to idolise. His big athletic body, his smooth delivery and immaculate line and length, plus his success on an international level, drove me on and on. There was always that secret hope that maybe one day I'd follow in Garth's footsteps. Freddie Trueman was an inspiration, too. Like Wes, he had that certain charisma for the young up-and-coming quickie . . . his aggression (he would snarl so meaningfully at the batsman if he was hit for four), his long run and fiery pace spurred me on. If you hit a four off Freddie you could expect some fireworks with the next ball and sometimes it was so mean that the batsman probably wished he had saved his boundary for the bowler at the other end. That was the way I wanted to bowl, it was the way I wanted to be regarded — fiery and aggressive, take no liberties with him, you never know what's coming next. Freddie had it all. Then there was Alan Davidson. He had the beautiful action and control, plus the rare ability to make the ball swing about at above average pace. They all helped me along the road without ever knowing how much. The memory of the impact these men made on me in my youth is a constant reminder to me that perhaps my example is being followed by others and I must continually raise my standards to set a good example. It is also the reason why I'm always ready to spend time with kids, because I remember so well the inspiration I got from the day I jumped the fence and 'met' an accommodating Wes Hall. I look at it this way: the kids of today are the pillars of the game tomorrow and we should all remember that. It doesn't take much to stop and give an autograph or a cheery word for a young lad. That sort of personal touch can have as much influence on a boy as all the great strokes you play or balls you bowl. I have little time for the prima donnas of sport who can't be bothered with the young fans who flock around them. They not only suffer from short memory, but short sightedness. Short memory in that they can't think back to the days when an autograph or a word would have meant the world to them, short-sightedness because they can't foresee the part the boys of today will play in their sport of tomorrow. Most kids are so enthusiastic for the sport that they can take a few set-backs from these prima donnas, but after a while they see little light in the dark and move on to other fields. A budding champion is lost to cricket.

From the very first days I have been almost fanatical about physical fitness. I guess this has come from the influence of my mother's father, Len Halifax, himself something of a country sportsman. He drummed into me an appreciation of the need for a sportsman to be really fit all the time. He used to say to me, 'If you can get your second wind and be in control of your body, then your mind will be free to cope with the job ahead.' It was wonderful advice and he rings me almost daily to remind me of it, but I know so well how true those words are that he really ought to save the money! During the school vacation when I was playing under-16s for South Belmont, I used to go and stay with Pop for special training. We would go running four times a week together and he used to drive me on and on. When you take a run-up as long as mine, you *must* be fit. Pop could appreciate that, and he has been my training adviser ever since. He used to really push me on until I reached the standard of fitness he thought I needed for my stints with the ball. Then he would hound me to make sure I kept my fitness at that level. I am eternally grateful for that training, because I am sure without it I would never have reached the levels of achievement I have.

In those days I was really dedicated to making something as a cricketer and, in fact, my dedication to sport grew to such proportions that in my early teens I found it hard to concentrate on schoolwork and began to look forward eagerly to the time when I could leave school and start work. After passing the examinations in my third year of senior schooling I gladly put school life behind me and took on a job as a clerk-storeman in a city warehouse. I had my sights set on a bank career, but I had to wait about six months before I realised this ambition. The early days with the South Belmont Club were hectic times for Trevor and me. Every Saturday we played with the juniors in the morning and then with the seniors in the afternoon. It was a sub-district competition and we played on concrete wickets coated by a strip of a bitumenised substance called malthoid. The club coach, Mick Basile, guided us along the way, but he finally realised it was time we graduated to senior district cricket with the nearby Perth Cricket Club. I was 16 at the time and I started my career with Perth in the second-grade side. The first game was nothing to get excited about. I took a couple of wickets on a wet wicket and scored 20-odd opening the batting. I spent most of that season in the seconds, but had the thrill of being chosen for the firsts late in the season. I took only one wicket in my first game and very few more for the remainder of the season. In those early days of first-grade cricket I was reasonably fast, but very, very inaccurate. I was playing on a very dead home ground wicket at Lathlain Park and was probably paying the penalty of trying too hard to get something out of the wicket.

It was about this stage that I first met the girl who was to become my wife. I guess I had shared the normal adolescent relationships with girls and had no idea of doing anything else but following this course when I went to the local delicatessen to buy some bread for my mother one evening. I was idly pondering over a rack of magazines when in walked an attractive young girl on a similar errand. I was immediately taken by her looks, even though I was only 17 and she was just 14 and still at school. I soon discovered that the pretty girl in the corner shop lived in the house directly behind ours in Carlisle, where we had recently moved from Belmont. It wasn't long before I had broken the ice and talked to young Helen Munsie. The relationship developed slowly, and we were married some three years later in 1970. I suppose at 20 and 17 we seemed a bit young to be married, but marriage had a wonderful steadying influence on me at a time when I needed to slow down and concentrate on making a go of cricket without all the side-tracks and pitfalls of being young and single. It must have been hard on Helen, because I put a lot into my cricket and she had to be very understanding as I was away from home often. Helen adjusted pretty well but it must have been a struggle as she knew nothing about cricket before meeting me. We bought our little house in East Victoria Park a month or so before we got married and have spent a lot of time renovating it. It has been a blissful relationship. The long periods when we have been apart through cricket have been difficult times but we have always written to each other every day. Immediately after my return from the West Indies in 1973 Helen fell pregnant with our first child but sadly she miscarried at 12 weeks. Happily five months later she became pregnant again.

It was in my early years with the Perth first-grade side that I came across another man who was to have an impact on my cricket make-up, captain Kevin Taylforth. He was not a great bowler, just a medium to medium-fast Saturday afternoon trundler who knew how to use his head, but he really hated the batsman and would do almost anything within his power to see him off. He was out there to win and it was no fault of his that we didn't win many more games in those days. That lesson was a good one for me . . . there's no point in playing cricket unless you really *want* to win. I didn't always relish doing the things he told me to do, like going back ready to bowl again if I had hit a batsman, but I know now that he was only trying to build within me a strong make-up that would stand me in good stead later. These were young, impressionable days and I'm thankful that Kevin's dogged attitude was there to be imprinted on my mind. Another to give me a gentle shove along was Peter Loader, the former Surrey and England fast bowler who had come to settle in Western Australia and had played a game or so with the Perth club before I arrived. Peter was always there if I needed help. He was soon snapped up by the WA Cricket Association to coach with the State Colts squad and he gave me a tremendous boost when he invited me to join the squad when I was still only 16. Most of the lads were in their late teens and early twenties, so it was a real injection for me.

I guess I've had more words of advice from well-meaning people since I started to emerge as a cricketer than anybody could imagine. I have always adopted the attitude that I would listen to everything they said and then sift through it and retain anything I felt would be of value. Plenty of times I have thrown it all away, but there have been the odd pearls that I have caught in the sieve just through taking the time and showing what I consider to be the courtesy to listen. An example of this came only recently, early in the 1973-4 season when I was committed to playing a season for Perth as a batsman and wasn't getting anywhere in my serious attempts with the bat. I was beginning to despair when I met a mate from a sub-district club, not much of a player at all. He suggested that as the bowler let the ball go I adopt a back-and-across motion to cover my stumps and give myself more time to play strokes. A couple of days later this advice was echoed by Basil Rigg, a former State player and an official at the Perth club, and I was on the way to a good season with the bat. Another casual conversation with a prominent sportsman resulted in a drastic change for the better in my physical training techniques. I was in the habit of attaining a good level of fitness through persistent and punishing long-distance runs. However, the message I got loud and clear from this conversation was that I could develop sharpness if I placed a far bigger emphasis on sprint work. It was top-quality advice and now I combine the two for maximum benefit from my time on the training track. There have been many similar examples of good bits of 'meat' left in the 'sieve' — but there have also been a few occasions when it has taken all my indulgence to refrain from being rude to people who come up to me and try to tell me their opinions. I think some of these people should save their opinions for discussions over a beer with a mate rather than weighing players down.

Of course, you don't even need the 'sieve' if you pick the right people to speak to, and if you're lucky enough to have them take an interest in you. I've learnt a mountain of advice from asking questions and listening to people like Richie Benaud, Ray Lindwall, Alan Davidson, Keith Miller and Wes Hall. These blokes are in no hurry to give you advice, unless, that is, you take time out to ask them. It makes me wonder just how much some top sportsmen are missing when they perhaps lack that bit of humility and a realisation that perhaps they could learn more by asking a few questions. In every walk of sporting life there are past champions, men who continue to make a study of the sport, who are over flowing with observations on the players of the day and ideas on how they could improve their game. Ray Lindwall, the former Australian fast bowling ace, is a great example of the past player who has kept in close contact with the game. He has been a wonderful adviser and friend to me ever since Christmas Day, 1971. Western Australia had a Christmas game against Queensland in Brisbane and Lindy invited Graham McKenzie, Rod Marsh, Ian Brayshaw and myself to his home for a wing-ding Christmas dinner. Lindy just has to be the best host in Brisbane. But he was so busy looking after his guests that it was a good couple of hours before I could do what I was itching to do, pin him down for a chat about my bowling. That was the beginning of a relationship I hope will last for ever. I had never seen Ray bowl, but I had read plenty about him and seen the odd film clip and I realise he must have been one of the very best. His readiness to help me then, and on many occasions since, puts him way up near the top of my all-time greats. He has written me umpteen letters, sometimes commenting on something he has seen just from watching me bowling on TV. Always it's a gentle suggestion here and there . . . just quiet, sincere Ray. Richie Benaud has always been a great help to me. Nothing, no request, has ever been too much and I'm most grateful that somebody of his standing in the cricket world has been bothered to even talk to me. He put me 'straight' three or four seasons ago when he saw me struggling a bit with my sharply-angled approach to the wicket. He apparently studied my bowling for some time, then offered me the advice that I try a more direct run-up. He suggested this would lay the foundations for pace, accuracy and an easier (on my body) action. I had originally come round a bit at the suggestion of Tony Lock, who thought at the time it would help develop an outswinger. Judging from results since, I think Richie was right. Alan Davidson is always a willing adviser on technical matters and the approach to fast bowling and Keith Miller, by his nature, is a forthright offerer of assistance whenever I ask him.

I had to do quite an apprenticeship in first-grade cricket before I finally got the Western Australian selectors 'nod' of approval to play for my State. In my fourth season of senior club cricket I began to settle down and learn a bit about the business of fast bowling. I finished well up on the association bowling list with 41 wickets at an average of 15.61. I was starting to get somewhere at last! At the start of the next season the Perth Cricket Club moved its headquarters, and a match between the club and the State team was played to celebrate the opening of the pavilion at Fletcher Park. My brother and I were both picked to play for Perth, and here Trevor did me as good a favour as he has ever done. We batted first with Trevor opening the innings and proceeding to hand out a real hiding to the State side's fast bowlers. He put up 40-odd in no time and this gave me great inspiration to do well against the State's best batsmen. I was almost jumping out of my skin when it came my turn to bowl. I was ready to set the world on fire, it was my big chance to do something classy when I was in the limelight and I wasn't about to waste the opportunity. As it turned out I didn't set the world on fire, but I did build up a bit of pace and I did bowl some outswingers — and the State selectors *were* there. I was very pleased at the end of the day and very grateful that I had a brother who knew when to take the bull by the horns.

3

There's always something dramatic about a major selection, if only for the person involved. But the circumstances of my selection to the State side for the first time were almost melodramatic! I was playing a club game on our home ground of Fletcher Park and the State team for the Eastern States tour was due to be announced on the radio at 5 o'clock that afternoon. Dad was at the ground as usual but today his attention was partly on our game and partly on the radio. I'd no real reason for believing that I might get a place, but State selections are not quite as predictable as some others, and your hopes start rising at a fairly early stage. On this particular occasion I was encouraged by the fact that Graham McKenzie and Laurie Mayne, WA's two best fast bowlers, were away in India with the Australian team and there seemed some chance for me, if only by default! Dad had promised that if I was named as a member of the team on the 5 o'clock announcement he'd signal by sounding the car horn.

The hour after tea break was endless. It was a suburban ground and there was no means of telling the time short of asking one of the umpires and I felt I could hardly do that every five minutes, much as I would have liked to. I have to confess that on several occasions I was on the point of asking and even tried to sneak a look at his watch as we changed between overs. One of the weaknesses of our plan was that we hadn't arranged for an alternative signal should the team be announced and my name not be in it. I was sure that the hour had gone by several times and had come to the conclusion that the team had been announced and that Dad had no means of telling me I had missed out. So I decided that I'd better get back to the game and forget all about State selection, at least for the time being. And then, as if from nowhere, came that raucous, beautiful, sound of a car horn. And then, not just one, but joining in and swelling the noise came every other car on the ground. I was in!

I was 20 years old and still not sure about my ability, but I realised the selectors had faith in me and I talked myself into believing that I was good enough. I was to make my debut away from home and had mixed feelings about that. I also had mixed feelings when I strained my left side in a club game a few days before we were due to leave for Brisbane. I was really sore from just under my arm down to my hip and the pain was aggravated when I brought my arm downwards in the delivery action. Should I go, should I stay? The question plagued me until the consequences became obvious: McKenzie and Mayne were away, this was my big chance and I had to grab it. I left with the team, determined to overcome my problems.

This was the first tour that I had been on and I tended to take everything at its face value. During the first day of the Brisbane game we were hit by a typical Brisbane down-

Dennis Lillee (17) with his brother Trevor (16) at the WACA Ground when both were members of the State Colts squad

Dennis Lillee during his first season for WA, 1969-70

Some of his WA teammates congratulating him on his first full Test selection for Australia. From left: Tony Mann, Les Varis, Bob Massie, Sam Gannon, Ross Edwards and Ken McAullay

Celebrations after WA had won the Sheffield Shield in the 1971-72 season. Ian Brayshaw, John Inverarity, Dennis Lillee, Sam Gannon and Derek Chadwick

The Rest of the World Match when he took eight wickets for 29 runs

ABOVE LEFT Indian Sunil Gavaskar gets a glove to the ball to be caught at the wicket by Rod Marsh

ABOVE RIGHT Bowling to Tony Greig . . .

. . . and the result. Keith Stackpole takes th catch at second slip

West Indian Clive
Lloyd in trouble

The last of the eight:
Clive Lloyd touches
the ball to Rod Marsh
behind the wickets

Dennis Lillee's superb bowling performance gives him the honour of leading the Australian team off the field, to the applause of teammates

Dennis Lillee being introduced to the Duke of Edinburgh by Graham McKenzie at the opening of a new cricket ground at the WA Institute of Technology

Two generations. The great English fast bowler Harold Larwood

Three generations. Having a drink on his return from England in 1972 with his father, Keith, and grandfather, Len Halifax

pour which literally flooded the Gabba ground. In the paper the following morning there was a photograph showing a beer can lying in the water with the scoreboard in the background showing Western Australia at 9-96. My mates in the team solemnly pursuaded me at breakfast that it was a 44-gallon drum, indicating that the ground had been some three feet under water! It certainly had rained hard and being the youngest member of the side and not willing to doubt the word of senior players, I naively believed every word. You can imagine how I felt when we eventually arrived at the ground and found it perfectly fit to play and with no evidence of the effects of all that rain! As our innings drew to a close that day I warmed up solidly outside the dressing-room before going in covered with sweat to make final preparations. I continued my vigorous warming up in the room as captain Tony Lock gave his address to the players. My teammates, who had no idea about my injury, were starting to wonder what sort of a bloke they had with them! Locky was like a father to me in those early games. I recall marking out my long run at the Brisbane Cricket Ground, all sorts of things racing through my mind and suddenly there was Locky standing there. His bald head was shining and there was that characteristic stance — and a characteristic piece of advice: 'Just bowl quick son and leave the rest to us.' That was Locky. I tried my best and built up a bit of pace in the first few overs, but it was a plumb wicket and I was guilty of spraying 'em about all over the place. I remember my first scalp very well. It was Sam Trimble, caught by Derek Chadwick fielding in close as usual. I also picked up Keith Dudgeon in that innings for figures of 2-60 from 17 overs. In the second innings I had the wicket of Mike Lucas at the cost of 16 runs from five overs. We lost on the first innings and narrowly failed to win outright.

I wasn't too happy with the way I had bowled. I suppose

every newcomer to a State side sees himself leading his beleaguered side from defeat to triumphant victory. The fact that we had lost the game had somewhat shattered this ideal. Locky understood all this. At the end of the match he grabbed a beer and we settled down in a corner of the dressing-room. For the next half hour or so he gave me the encouragement I needed to look forward to the rest of the tour with confidence. Locky was welcome company then and on many occasions since. But it wasn't always easy with the old master. He was so blunt and uncompromising. He wasn't one to beat around the bush. He had learnt the hard way as a professional in the tough school of county cricket. I think all those tough times he had as a junior pro were stamped indelibly on his mind and he wasn't about to give any youngster an easy path through his early years. Locky had no time for any bowler who pretended to be fast, but wasn't. In my early days he never criticised me for my inaccuracy as long as I was building up pace. I vividly recall the old fox coming up to me in the middle of an over in one of my early games and saying, 'Can't you bowl faster than that? That's pathetic!' I'm sure he was just trying to spur me on and I guess he did just that, because I tried my hardest to show the old master that I could do it, that I could be faster than his flaming Trueman and Tyson! I guess he got what he wanted out of me, but I had to conceal the fact that it hurt me to have to be spoken to like that by my captain. Actually, his goadings and cajolings remind me of a story I once heard about Wes Hall and Charlie Griffith in their heyday. Apparently the West Indies players used to get an extra yard or two out of both of them by going up to one after the other and saying, 'Gee you're a bit off today, Wes (or Charlie) is bowling the pants off you . . . he's yards faster!' I'm told that had the desired effect of really hotting it up for the batsmen.

Locky set the standard of dedication to the task at the

highest level — and it was up to each of his men to endeavour to live up to that standard. That was no easy task, which probably explains why there wasn't too much praise floating about during the Lock era. I think the most important thing about Locky was that he gained the respect of his men — and his opponents. From my experience, that respect made me try that little bit harder, for Locky, rather than for myself or even for WA. Before I was chosen to play for WA I was acutely aware of the aura that surrounded the old master. I had seen him play at the WACA Ground and in club games and had a fair appreciation of the appeal, the charisma of the man. Immediately I played in the same team with him I sensed an air of expectancy each time he was on the field. I guess that's what made him so popular with the crowds. They knew that whenever Locky was around, there was a really good chance something would happen. It might be a brilliant catch, a raucous appeal, a few lusty strokes or a tantalising piece of spin bowling. Maybe it was because he had played so much by the time I joined him in the first-class cricket arena, but Locky always seemed to have everything under control when he came on to bowl. He had the fieldsmen that little bit more on their toes, for fear that they might make an error when Locky was bowling, and he most certainly had the power to bewitch and bewilder batsmen. I'm sure I've seen batsmen leave the ground shaking their heads in wonderment at how Locky managed to get them out, some of them almost glad they'd finished their session of his particular brand of slow torture. Locky bowled as though he expected to take a wicket with every ball, and how often he did! His performance in taking 326 wickets for WA, at the remarkable average of 24.69 and excellent (for a finger spinner in Australia) striking rate of a wicket every 8.6 overs, tells the story. The only time I remember Locky getting some hammer was at the hands of New South Wales batsman Tony

Steele when he scored 123 on the WACA in 1970. Locky set out to buy Steele's wicket, tossing a few up with men liberally sprinkled around the boundary. Steele was in fine touch and kept on hitting Locky either out of reach or over the line. The old fox finally had his way, Ross Edwards catching Steele on a mis-hit, but it had cost Locky far more than he would have liked.

Locky was at his very best bowling at newcomers. Those who had been around for a while seemed to play him with far more caution, but the newcomers, noticing that the great Tony Lock didn't seem to be spinning the ball very much, inevitably took liberties. That was right up Locky's alley. He started to weave a web and in the end there was no way out.

Locky had his favourites among the regular tail-enders on the circuit, like Queensland's Ross Duncan and NSW's Dave Renneberg. He would 'butter them up' beautifully, chatting to them before the game, when they came in to bat and in the dressing-room — after their scalp had been added to his list. It was the same old story each time . . . a man at long on, a man at long off and don't bother where the rest are stationed. Then Locky would send down three or four really tight, flat deliveries on the stumps, which would have his man scrambling to keep the ball out. After their 'indoctrination', plus the odd quip down the wicket, Locky would move in at the same pace, but let the ball go well behind the crease and way up in the air — it was too much and the end result was a catch in the deeps. One day a hapless farmer boy playing in a Country versus City match got off-side with Locky. The country side was battling to get a few runs on the board and the old fox wasn't trying too hard to knock them over. In fact, he was sending up juicy full-tosses one after another in an effort to tempt this batsman to hit out and put a few runs on the board. But the country player had heard about

Locky and obviously thought he was sending down hand grenades, because he just blocked and padded away these full tosses till in the end the old master got fed up. Enough was enough. Locky loaded up, went wide of the crease, cocked his elbow the slightest bit, and fired out perhaps the fastest ball that had been bowled all day. The ball had careered into the stumps before the farmer had even lifted his bat to its maximum height. As the dazed batsman went past Locky on his way back to the pavilion, the old fox gave him such a stare, as much as to say: 'Well, I gave you the chance to take a few runs, you wouldn't take it, so off you go.'

Locky was a great one for a little bit of gamesmanship — and he was at his very best when things got embarrassingly tight in a knockout match for WA in Launceston against Tasmania in 1970. The Warwickshire player, Billy Ibadullah, was on a coaching contract in Tasmania and was captain of the local side, who were making a really good show of things against their mainland opponents. Billy had opened the batting, but retired hurt fairly early in the proceedings. Tasmania had gone from strength to strength in Billy's absence and when the third wicket fell at 151, only 67 runs short of the WA total, the Warwickshire player thought he would return to the crease to ensure an easy stroll to victory. The attack was flagging a bit and Billy might have taken control of things but Locky wouldn't have a bar of it. He said Ibadullah couldn't return to the crease at that early stage. The local officials raced from pillar to post checking the rule books and finally a decision was reached: Ibadullah could return to the crease. Locky was visibly most upset. He stood for some seconds with his arms clenched across his chest in defiance, and you could tell he had made a decision to get rid of this 'intruder'. He immediately called Graham McKenzie into the attack, set the most ridiculous attacking field with men all round the bat and, first ball, out went Billy. Locky had decided this man deserved no better, and he just told Garth: 'Knock him over.' It was a wonderful piece of one-upmanship that turned the game and we won by 13 runs.

Locky was so old and tough that he almost had barnacles on him. But he was the centre of entertainment wherever we played in Australia. He was the darling of the Hill mob in Sydney, the target for a tirade of friendly jibes from crowds everywhere. He brought something to West Australian and Australian cricket that very few others could do. That was simply personality. He was the cricket entertainer extraordinaire. He was a tough player and leader, but underneath it all he was a great guy. At the end of a day's play he would grab a glass, a bottle of beer and seek out the youngest player in the opposition to spend an hour talking with him about cricket.

From Brisbane we went down to Sydney for the next game on the tour. I was instructed to share a cabin with John Inverarity and it was the first time I had been inside a sleeper cabin on a train. The bottom bed was visible, being used as the seat in the carriage, but the top bunk was tucked away out of sight and actually formed the backrest of the seat. Way up the top of the carriage was the luggage rack, about two feet wide and made of slats of wood. Inverarity, sensing I wasn't aware that the second bunk was hidden away, quickly told me he was the senior player and entitled to have the bottom bunk. The top bunk, he said, was mine. He pointed to the luggage rack, much to my horror. He gave no hint of the trick when I protested and I was trying to squeeze onto the rack before Invers, unable to contain himself any longer, burst out laughing.

My first visit to the Sydney Cricket Ground was a disappointment. The wicket was yards slower than those I was to meet at that ground later and on this occasion figures of 4-81 and 0-13 were nothing to write home about. It was a similar story on the uncompromising turf in Melbourne where I took 1-71 and 1-27. Adelaide was the last stop for us on that tour and it was the scene of one of my least charming performances on the cricket field. The incident involved umpire Freddie Godson, a very pleasant little chap who most certainly didn't deserve the fate which befell him. It was an extremely hot day and I had been bowling for some time in trying conditions. I was breathing mainly through my mouth, which had become very parched. Suddenly as I let a delivery fly a denture plate in my mouth almost fell out. I thought it might fly out on the pitch if I kept going, so I decided the best thing to do was to give it to the umpire. I hastily removed the plate, hoping nobody would see, and walked up to Freddie Godson with it in my hand. 'Would you mind keeping this for me,' I said, handing him the plate. He didn't really look at what I was giving him until it was in his hand, then he looked at it a second time with horror written all over his face. He didn't know what to do with it for some seconds, then finally he took a handkerchief from his pocket and wrapped it up and rather thankfully hid it away in the depths of his jacket pocket!

I took six wickets in Adelaide bringing my total for the tour to 15, and I was a sorely disillusioned player when we arrived back in Perth. I was moping around the WA Cricket Association Ground one practice afternoon soon after the tour when I ran into Laurie Mayne's father, who gave me a big lift when he said my 15 wickets on tour was a very good performance. 'If you take 15 wickets in the East you'll end up with more than 30 for the season,' he said. I thought he was just trying to boost my morale, but soon it occurred to me that he was dead right. And I later realised that it had been probably a good thing for me to play my first few games away from the Perth ground, which notoriously favours the pace bowlers. I had endured the Eastern States tour on deadpan wickets, but I had learnt a lot in those four games. After the tour I took something of a knock when I was relegated to 12th man for the first home game — a knockout match against South Australia. I was told while bowling in the nets about 20 minutes before the game was due to start and it was such a sharp shock to me that the next three or four balls I bowled nearly decapitated the poor batsman down at the other end.

Perhaps the selectors had got wind of my side injury and wanted me to have a short rest, because I was back in the team for the next four-day game, a Shield match, also against South Australia and also in Perth. South Australia won the toss and batted into the 200s with me making little contribution to our cause, taking only one wicket out of the first nine. Towards the end of their innings Locky took the new ball in an attempt to break a stand between Lance Gibbs and South Australian No. 11 Trevor Pearson. Pearson, a very pleasant chap, was their fast bowler and at No. 11 was not a noted batsman! But he was holding his end well and enabling Gibbs to continue scoring. This was my first home game for WA and I felt it was up to me to do something about it. Unfortunately, the results were not what I intended as the combination of this tension and the newness of the ball produced a string of dangerous deliveries to Pearson before I finally bowled him to end their innings. I was appalled at what I had done as I had broken one of the most important unwritten rules of cricket. Nobody spoke to me as I walked off the field and as I reached the dressing-room I decided to go and apologise to Pearson and the South Australian captain, Les Favell. As I entered the visitors' rooms the usual noisy chatter faded into a hostile silence. Unnerved, I stumbled through an apology to Pearson, Favell and the South Australian team, but this brought a tirade of abuse from Favell, who was obviously very upset. His anger triggered mine as I felt he might at least have given me some credit for trying to make the apology and I suddenly felt after all the unpleasantness a need to reassert myself. Perhaps I slightly overdid it, because I told Favell that he'd better watch out next time I was bowling to him and stormed out of the room with my rage giving way to fear at the enormity of what I had done. I reported the matter to Locky, who immediately gave me a bigger dressing-down than had Favell. Locky told me I had no right to speak so rudely to an opposing player, let alone to the captain and a man of such experience and standing as Favell. I was mortified. Somehow I staggered to my corner of the room and slumped into my seat. John Inverarity saved the day when he came up and consoled me, saying he thought I had done the right thing in the circumstances. I got 7-36 in the second innings and Favell was one of them, caught in the slips for eight. Les and I share a joke about that incident now, but I thought it was the end of the world then.

The season ended on a quiet note for me, but I was WA's top wicket-taker for the season with 32 victims at an average of 22.03 and a striking rate of a wicket every six overs. That was good enough, apparently, for me to be picked for the Australian second team for the tour of New Zealand under Sam Trimble. It was something I hadn't dared think about, Australian selection at the end of my first season of first-class cricket, and I was extremely excited about the prospects when we left Sydney for New Zealand. Geoff Davies, the New South Wales batsman, and I were the two left out for the opening match against Canterbury at Christchurch. We were both so excited about being away on our first tour that after nets each morning we took off for a long run together to keep our fitness at peak and to run off some of our nervous energy. Alan 'Froggy' Thomson (Victoria) and Dave Renneberg (New South Wales) pipped me for the fast bowling berths in the first two Tests against the Kiwis. But I was chosen to lead the attack in the final Test at Wellington. It was a real batsman's wicket. Trimble scored 213 and Bevan Congdon made 128, both collecting their runs as though they were batting against schoolboys. My one victim for the match was Glen Turner, caught at the wicket for five. My figures for the match were 21 overs, six maidens, one wicket for 92 runs. Not exactly an auspicious opening to my career as an international bowler.

I played in four matches on the tour and it was a great experience. One consolation was my batting, where I finished well up on the tour averages, once out for 47 runs. I went home with 18 victims next to my name at a pleasing average of 16.44 at a striking rate of a wicket every five overs

How New Zealand cricket has advanced since that 1970 tour! Australia had never played a full Test against New Zealand and this tour was a continuation of that stance between the two countries. Now the Kiwis have proven their worth in series in the West Indies, England, Australia and against the Aussies in New Zealand, where they won a Test against the full Australian eleven. That was a great blow to the Australian pride, but it must have done a lot of good for the game in New Zealand, and the Kiwis now have confidence in themselves. In 1970 we found them to be sadly lacking in self-confidence. Even though we were only the Australian second team, we felt they looked up to us as being a cut and a half above them. When we got together after play the New Zealanders would gather around us like schoolchildren, eager to ask questions, eager to learn from their 'teachers'. Now it is evident that they were simply picking our brains to better themselves for a bright future. They have arrived as a cricketing nation and now we can look to more regular interchanges, and that can only be for the good of the game in both countries.

Bad weather followed us around the country in 1970 and the wickets generally did not favour fast bowlers. But I floated around from city to city, lapping it all up and learning something at every turn. It was good grounding and I returned to Perth a far better State player for it. I was able to approach the 1970-71 season without having worry about my place in the State side, although with the return of Graham McKenzie to the side I had to concede the use of the wind.

I had a terrible Eastern States tour, taking only six wickets in four games for plenty of runs. Then we had the Barry Richards debacle in the first home game against SA in November. Again I opened the bowling into the wind, and the sea breeze at the Perth ground can play havoc with the rhythm and stamina of a medium-pacer, let alone a quickie. Richards played so well. The first ball McKenzie bowled to him beat the South African outside the off stump and I can't recall seeing another ball beat the bat until he missed a full toss and was out lbw to leg-spinner Tony Mann for 356. I remember him being dropped at mid-on when he was about 160 and, as I recall, there wasn't such a to-do about the missed chance. I guess we all thought he wouldn't last too much longer, but he lasted for about 200 more runs! Again I put in a poor performance, none for 117, and I was beginning to lose some of that confidence I had gained on the New Zealand tour.

My stocks hit rock bottom a week or so later when the team for the game against the MCC was announced and I was 12th man. I must admit things were going so badly that I thought it was the end of a brief career for

Dennis Lillee. I naturally thought the next step for me would be out of the 12 and perhaps the end of the road. But I got a reprieve when Graham McKenzie dropped out of the game and I was brought back into the line-up — and given the use of the wind. The two things combined to bring a breath of fresh air into my life. I was on top of the world again and went into the game full of vigour and vitality. The first ball I bowled knocked Geoff Boycott's cap off. It was pretty fast and the first couple of overs were generally yards faster than I had bowled all season. But then I was struggling again. I ended the innings with no wickets next to my name, just a pleasant memory of having shaken Mr Boycott's confidence. It didn't take him long to get over that . . . he and Brian Luckhurst both scored centuries in a 215-run opening stand. I went home that night in a condition again approaching despair about my future as a cricketer.

I had done little to deserve the reprieve I had been given, but there was to be another stroke of luck. I went out for the second innings relaxed, resigned to the fact that it was just a matter of bowling out time and then packing my bags for good. It was the right formula. I just let myself go and picked up Colin Cowdrey in my first spell for six and Boycott later in the innings for nine. I had turned the corner. After the game Jack Fingleton went into print saying he thought I should be tried in the Tests — just because I had bowled pretty fast. It was just the fillip I needed. It gave me a shove in the right direction, a hope for the future. The present started to look after itself as in the next game, against Queensland in Perth, I teamed up with Bob Massie for the first time that season and we took 14 wickets between us for the match, six of them mine.

It wasn't the figures I was so pleased about, more a satisfaction within myself that I was again bowling with verve and fire. I knew I was essentially a with-the-wind bowler and I needed that breeze on my shoulders. The season finished sweetly. Wickets kept on tumbling my way and soon I was blinking in amazement and disbelief at seeing my name up for the Sixth Test against England at the Adelaide Oval.

4

In Western Australia there is an annual match between the Metropolitan (or State) side and a Country Eleven in Perth. It falls on the Sunday in the middle of the country-week carnival when teams from all over the State pour into the city to pit themselves in a rapid flurry of their favourite summer sport. The big game is played on the WACA Ground and although the city side invariably wins it does give the country boys something to look forward to each year. I'm sure they get a big thrill out of being chosen to face up against the State's best bowlers and to trundle a few down against the best batsmen.

I suppose there was the usual amount of excitement amongst the country players in January 1971 when their names went up on the blackboard in the bar at the WACA Ground. To me the game represented an enjoyable Sunday's toil. Perhaps I wouldn't be able to bowl flat out as country batsmen just don't come up against much true pace and you have to be a bit careful. But there was to be another kind of thrill for me during that 1971 Metropolitan verus Country game. The City side batted first and had little trouble collecting a score that would keep our Country opponents at bay. Things were as normal as you would expect in a team dressing-room until the announcement came over the radio that the Australian team for the next Test had been chosen and that I was in it. All of a sudden that room was anything but normal as people streamed in to offer me their congratulations. I was really on cloud nine. Helen was at home when the team was announced, but she raced to the ground to congratulate me at the tea break. What a proud time it was. My parents and grandfather were already at the ground and I was thrilled to be able to share the moment with them.

I had everything to gain and absolutely nothing to lose. I was the fifth fast bowler to have been tried by the selectors in that series, so I really couldn't fail. At least I had been chosen for a Test match and that had been one of my earliest goals in cricket. Now it had arrived and I could barely believe it. I was still way up in the air when we went out to bowl at the country side. The result was most embarrassing for me and the other members of the city team. I bowled like a raw third-grader. No matter how hard I tried, I couldn't concentrate long enough to even hold a good line, let alone build up a bit of pace. I have often wondered what those few hundred people who were at the ground that day must have thought of me. I hope that they understood.

Before I left for Adelaide with Rod Marsh, WA's only other representative in the Australian team, I gave a lot of thought to what lay ahead of me. A Test match . . . against England . . . what was it going to be like? . . . what could I expect? A thousand questions raced through my mind. In the Press I was being built up as Australia's answer to John Snow in the 'bumper war' that had developed during the series. That began to weigh on me until I met Sir Donald Bradman at a function in Adelaide before the game. I was talking to Sir Charles Gairdner, the former Governor of Western Australia, when Sir Donald approached me. The legendary batting champion butted in briefly to say he woud like to see me before I left. When our conversation ended Sir Donald and I went aside from the group and sat down together for a while. He told me: 'You have been picked for Australia to bowl how you normally would. Forget about this "bumper war" business. Just keep the ball well up to the batsman and bowl normally and I'm sure you will do well.' That was some of the best advice I have ever received in cricket. It was so sensible because I was too young and 'green' to get involved in a bumper war and to have tried could have been fatal to my cricket future. Apart from the fact that you lose effect if you try to bowl too many bumpers, there is also the fact that the wicket at the Adelaide Oval is about the last place in the world where you'd want to try that sort of a plan in a Test match. Sir Donald's words were with me throughout the game. I am truly grateful that he took the time to offer them to me.

My most vivid memory of the opening stages of the game was a strange 'colour-contrast' sensation as we walked out onto the Adelaide Oval to start the game. I was walking near the rear of the Australian team and I recall being struck almost dumb by an awesome contrast between the pearly-white creams of the players ahead of me and the lush green of the oval surface. It was an eerie experience, the colours were so vivid and strong in the bright Adeaide sunshine.

The pressure was taken off me slightly by the fact that 'Froggy' Thomson, the wrong-foot Victorian quickie, took the first over of the game. It gave me time to regain some composure, but it did mean I had to come up into the wind. I struggled those early overs. I seized up a bit, found little pace and only ordinary degrees of line and length. It wasn't going to be easy, this Test cricket. I had to wait a long time for first 'blood' — England were 1-276 (Geoff Boycott run out for 58) when I finally struck pay dirt by having John Edrich caught at slip. It was a lazy stroke at a ball pitched outside the off stump, but I guess Edes was entitled to play a tired stroke. He was out for 130, caught by Keith Stackpole. I went to bed that night reasonably happy with my figures of 1-41 from 14 overs, pleased that I had taken my first Test wicket, but not overjoyed about the way I had bowled. It was a slow wicket and I had shown little sign of penetration.

The next morning was a turning point for me. I was given the use of the wind and immediately the ball started to swing away from the righthanders. Suddenly I was calling the tune. Everything I tried came off. It was an exhilarating feeling. I was bowling with ease and rhythm. Perhaps I had just needed that first day to settle my nerves. I got England's nightwatchman, Alan Knott, early on and later in the day bowled Ray Illingworth with a ball I'll never forget. It started on the line with the stumps, started to move out a bit, then bit back off the pitch and clean bowled him. I must admit it was an absolute fluke. Wouldn't it be nice to be able to bowl them whenever you wanted to! I added the wickets of John Snow and Bob Willis for innings figures of 5-84 off 28.3 overs. I was beside myself with joy. Richie Benaud wrote: 'I could see a different bowler today from the one I saw yesterday.' That night I was a different man, too, because I let my hair down and had a few drinks with the lads at a barbecue. Rod Marsh took me under his wing and we had quite a few sips together — thank goodness we had a free day the following day! Among all the celebrations I took time out to curse myself for having talked my father out of driving the long distance (about 1500 miles) from Perth to Adelaide to see me in my first Test match. How proud he would have been.

As the game progressed the wicket died right down — as is normally the way on the 'graveyard' at the Adelaide Oval. In the second innings there was little going for the quickies and I didn't add to my tally for the game. In the week between the Sixth and Seventh Tests WA played Queensland in the Knockout Cup final in Melbourne, won the match and the right to shoot up to Sydney and play against the MCC. In that game, on a pretty dicey rain-affected wicket, a ball from Graham McKenzie reared up and struck Geoff Boycott on the arm and broke a bone. This put Geoff out of the Test the following week. The giant Queenslander Tony Dell took Thomson's place in the Australian team and I was able to open the attack with the wind.

But Sydney was a match I'd rather forget. It was a complete reversal of form for me. I was guilty of trying to bowl too fast. I bowled only one decent ball in the match — and that yorked Illingworth to have him lbw in the second innings. My figures for the first innings were 1-32 off 13 overs, for the second 2-43 from 14 overs. But I was just all over the place, seemingly without rhyme or reason.

In the second innings Ian Chappell, who had been appointed captain of the side to replace Bill Lawry, sent me in as a night-watchman and I saw out the few deliveries till the end of play. The next morning Ian came up to me and told me he was grateful for what I had done the night before and now I could resume my normal position in the batting order. I thought this was a bit odd, but this *was* a Test match and Ian Chappell *was* the Australian captain, so I didn't hurry back from the nets for the start of play, preferring to use the time there having a good workout. The umpires had gone onto the ground before Ian realised I had taken him seriously and he had to send a runner out to get me to come to the dressing-room and prepare to continue my innings. Boy, was I gullible!

It was after this game that I first had thoughts of going to England to play cricket for a season. I spoke at length on the matter with Boycott in the dressing-room before returning to Perth. He suggested I try out some of the county clubs and even wrote a couple of letters for me. This came to nothing, but it had started me thinking and before long I secured a contract to play for Haslingden in the Lancashire League.

It was the first time out of Western Australia for Helen and she was particularly excited when we went out to Perth Airport to meet two other WA couples also on their way to play in the British Leagues. They were Tony Mann and his wife, Lyn, and Bruce Yardley and his wife, Kath. Tony was to play for Bacup also in the Lancashire League and Bruce was bound for Perth in Scotland. We had decided to have a short holiday on the way over and the six of us spent a couple of wonderful days in Hong Kong and two more in Zurich. As we flew the short leg from Zurich to London Helen and I began to feel anxious. We had no idea what to expect in the busy five months to follow and we were concerned about our immediate arrangements once we parted company with our friends and were left to our own resources. Tension mounted as we circled and came in to land at Heathrow Airport, the lights of London making an incredible pattern of jewels below us. From Heathrow we had our first ride in a double-decker bus into the city, and crossed to Euston Station, where we were to catch a train to Manchester. As arranged, we rang Tom Lees, the secretary of the Haslingden club, to get further instructions on how to find our way round Euston Station. We had to wait a couple of hours before the train was due to leave and were so reluctant to leave our baggage that I sat on one of the cases in the waiting room while Helen went to buy us some food. Tom Lees and his wife and another club supporter, Joss Knowles, met us at Piccadilly Station in Manchester. We had finally arrived. The tensions were over and we were in safe hands.

Two things stood out in the trip from the station to our digs in Haslingden. We were taken aback at the dingy state of the buildings we passed on the way and staggered by the fact that English drivers weren't using headlights even though it was near midnight. We were taken to a comfortable semi-detached home backing onto a playing field which I was happy to use regularly for physical training during my stay. All seemed well when our new friends departed later that night, but what a shock it must have been for Tom Lees to hear from me bright and early the next morning! I had to report that the double bed set aside for us had broken and there was a very strange silence at the other end of the line! The following night we were introduced to the club at a special function and Helen and I were deeply impressed by the immediate warmth of the Lancastrians. Then it was down to hard work, for me and them! It was my first experience as a coach, I was only 20 and some of my men were twice my age and more. I went about it the only way I knew and that was to run and get fit. Some of the boys took a while to get used to my sort of training routines, but finally most of them joined in whenever I ordered a session of physical training. One thing Helen and I found hard to accept was the training hours. We had been used to training back home at 5 o'clock and finishing when the sun set at about 7.30. Now we had to get used to practice sessions starting at 6.30 and finishing about 9.30, and to sitting down to our evening meal at 10 o'clock or later.

The club got me at job in a local rock quarry doing weighbridge ticketing. That was pretty hectic for a couple of weeks but then things slowed down at the quarry and I was able to coast through the rest of my employment there. Helen started work immediately with a big local trucking firm as a secretary.

There's no doubting the substance of Lancashire League cricket and it all stems from the people of the area. They are so dedicated that they'll turn out on the worst of days just to see their team in action. The numbers at each game aren't anywhere near as high as in the great days of the Leagues just after the War, but the crowds are just as keen. To take a stroll around the Bent Gate ground at Haslingden, Lanehead at Bacup or Alexander Meadows at Blackburn during a League game is to see the very salt of Britain. It never ceased to amaze me just how keen Lancastrians are for their cricket. I've played in club games in Western Australia between two sides boasting a line-up of half a dozen Test and State cricketers who would be very welcome as professionals in the Lancashire League and yet they have been no more than Saturday afternoon club games. But put together 22 cricketers, with only two such international or interstate stars and often a complement of players with far less appeal and make the scene a quaint ground in the League area and you've got a whole new kettle of fish. There is a fresh atmosphere about things, the handful of spectators becomes hundreds or even thousands and there is a real game on. It was a wonderful experience playing in the League and I learnt a lot in the 25 or so games that I played for Haslingden. Sure it was hard work adjusting to the slower wickets and occasionally there were times I would have given a lot to have been able to pack it in and go home, but there was something new and exciting around every corner and we had a fabulous time. One thing I learned in the League is that you've got to look after yourself. Early on in proceedings the groundsman at Haslingden explained to me that he would shave the grass right off the wicket for me, so it would be hard and fast like he had heard they were in Australia. When I got out to bowl on it I found the ball was coming off so slowly I might as well have been a spinner. Indeed, our off-spinner, John Ingham, was doing just fine, turning them quite a bit and getting a haul each week. A few games went by and I began to notice I was doing far better away from home on wickets with a little bit of grass on them. Suddenly it dawned on me— Ingham, an old hand in the Leagues, had been getting into the groundsman's ear and ordering the sort of wicket he personally wanted, and never mind about the professional! I fronted the groundsman, who coughed up the plot and we finally struck a compromise: He would shave the wicket at one end for Jack and leave plenty of grass at the other for me.

Indeed it's not at all unusual for factors other than the elements to interfere with the playing conditions at most, if not all, the League grounds. How could I ever forget my one and only game at Rawtenstall, who had the South Australian, Terry Jenner, a leg-spinner, as their professional. I had given the Rawtenstall batsmen a bit of a shake-up on our pitch the week before and we were really looking forward to getting stuck into them in the return match. There hadn't been a drop of rain for a week, believe it or not, and we were a happy lot as we travelled in the team bus the few miles from Haslingden to Rawtenstall. However, our spirits took a dramatic tumble when we arrived to find the wicket saturated, particularly around the bowler's footholds. There was no way in the world I could bowl fast and I just skated over the ground every time I tried!

Cricket followers in England are a type all of their own. They study the game far more than any others I have come across and they have a wonderful memory for players of the past. Dig out an old fellow in the crowd at Headingley and ask him about a few recent players and his eyes will mist over as he tells you about Wilf Rhodes or Len Hutton as though he had seen him in action only half an hour ago. Memories are possibly even better among the stalwarts of the Lancashire League. I think it's because the hero worship there has been for the professionals, and when you consider that the line-up of fast visitors includes Leary Constantine, Ray Lindwall, Everton Weeks, Wes Hall, Bob Simpson, Eddie Barlow and Ian Chappell there's no wondering why.

One Australian player who is bound to go down in the annals of the Lancashire League as one of its greats is Neil Hawke. The former South Australian and Australian all-rounder has become quite a legend in the League through his long and almost-uniquely successful stint there. Hawkey married a girl from Leeds and settled in Lancashire some years ago and he really looks forward to the Australian pros coming over each summer so that he can renew acquaintances and catch up with the news from home. In his own way he is something of a father figure to the Aussies in the League. He works on the theory that you play to win, no doubt about that, but when a young Aussie bobs up you sort of ease him into things. I was aware that he would perhaps give me a couple well up to get off the mark, and I was aware that he would expect something similar in return. Haslingden batted first and, true to form, Hawkey threw one up which, before I gave it a thought, I smacked over the fence for six. The look of shock on Neil's face at that moment was beaten only by the glare I got from the old warrior when I greeted his arrival at the crease later in the day with a bouncer that just grazed his right ear. Both acts were unintentional, but to this day Hawkey still has his doubts about me.

Not that you got much value from bowling short stuff. Perhaps the most important thing I learnt during my stay in the League was the need to bowl good line and length on the wet and soft wickets. I couldn't build up much pace, because I was never confident about my footing and anything short of a length is easy pickings for even the weakest of batsmen. The ball just sits up and hangs in the air, waiting to be smacked away for four. It was the first year of the League's trial period with limited-overs games and in the first half of the season we were on the wrong end in a lot of games that only just went one way or the other. When we settled down later in the season we won more than we lost, but all we could do was rise from the bottom to finish 11th. Batting was really hard work. I started in the middle order and just couldn't get going during the first half of the season and produced a string of failures. In the second half I started to adjust to the slow wickets and indeed my last innings for Haslingden was 48 — run out just two runs short of a collection around the ground, but it did win me a bat from the property-man of the club, Dave McQuade. Dave had been nursing this particular bat along throughout my stay. It was my bat and he oiled it and prepared it with loving care each week. Nobody else could touch it, which was a pity because it didn't get much use from me. Before the final game started Dave made the grand offer: 'If you score more than 30 with this bat, it's yours.'

I took 68 wickets at 13-85 and scored 207 runs which was far from outstanding when compared with the figures of the coloured South African Dik Abed, who scored 662 runs and took 101 wickets in carrying his team Enfield to a League title. But we had some good times and I think they were reasonably happy with me at Haslingden. Helen and I made some lasting friendships and still correspond regularly with people who looked after us so well during our stay.

Apart from the splendid people we met during our stay, the one thing that really appealed to me was the variety of grounds in the League. Each had its own individuality and above all there was a wonderful atmosphere embracing each ground, no matter how bad the weather, how dull the cricket or how small the crowds. Because most of the League area is in and around the Pennine mountain chain that runs down the middle of England, a good percentage of the grounds were far from being level. But none was as 'wonky' as the ground at Colne. There was a drop of at least 10 feet from one end to the other, which was all very well for the man bowling downhill (usually the professional), but very hard work for the poor bloke at the other end. The day I played there with Haslingden in 1971 we played on the bottom wicket, so close to the pavilion boundary that a mis-hit block would pierce the field for a four, or six! On the other side, higher up-the-hill the boundary was so far away as to be beyond the reach of even the most powerful hitters. I was operating with the slope and starting my run near a colossal fowlhouse backing onto the ground. We were doing quite well, picking up a few wickets here and there, until somebody opened up the fowlhouse and a stench which literally took the wind out of us drifted across the ground and left us in no mood to continue the destruction until the air cleared some minutes later.

It was cricket, work, cricket for most of the time, but we bought a car and spent all our spare time touring. We visited North Wales, Coventry, Sherwood Forest, the Lake District and of course had a thorough look at Lancashire. One of our sorties away from home involved a run up to Scotland. The club gave us a week off training and we went straight to Perth and stayed for a couple of days with the Yardleys, then took them across to Kilmarnock for the wedding of my State team colleague and friend, Bob Massie, to a local Scots lass called Nancy Coulthard. On arriving in Kilmarnock we went straight to the ground where we met the Manns and settled down for a few pints and a bit of Australian barracking for Bob, who was playing in a twilight match. At the wedding we also met up with Laurie Mayne, who was playing for Greenock, and his wife Jackie. The Australian contingent for the big occasion was bolstered by Bob's father and his sister. We soon found that the Scots had plenty in mind for us. They wanted to see us topped up with Scotch and they spent the best part of the evening trying to achieve that and the rest of the time making sure their own glasses were never empty. Helen compromised by drinking a weak mixture of Scotch and lemonade, but they succeeded with me. It was a great night!

As the season drew to a close Helen and I were saddened by the thought that we would possibly never see these fine people again. There were many who had done all they could to make our stay happy and memorable and we were both extremely grateful to them. I was lucky enough to return to my old haunts when I was in England in 1972 with the Australian team. There were a couple of memorable re-unions and I hope there will be more in the future.

Back in Perth I had to settle down again and consolidate my place in the Australian side. And that wasn't going to be easy, no matter how you looked at it. If I had thought of taking a sigh of relief when it was announced that the South African side, boasting such batting champions as Barry Richards and Graham Pollock, would not tour Australia, then I had another thought coming. The Herald and Weekly Times newspaper group stepped in and promoted an alternative touring team called The Rest of the World, an impressive line-up of the 'best of the rest', led by the greatest of the greats, Gary Sobers. This promotion was a blessing for Australian cricket, because it would have been a tragedy if we had not played a series that summer. Ian Chappell was just in the process of building a respectable Australian team and we needed matches together in preparation for the big trial: England in 1972.

The Sheffield Shield season opened in unspectacular

fashion for me as I had the modest return of 10 wickets from our first two home games and had not been greatly pleased with my form. It was during the second game, against Victoria, that I bowled the fastest ball of my life. We were hot in pursuit of outright victory, elated by our luck in running Bill Lawry out for a duck after he had scored a painstaking century in the first innings. Victoria's No. 7 batsman was Peter Bedford, a champion Australian Rules footballer but a quiet and nice bloke (why is it always the nice guys I get tangled up with?). Bedford had been on the brink of Australian selection a couple of seasons before, but at this time was palpably out of form. We had knocked him over for three in the first innings and he was looking anything but safe in the second innings when he snicked one off me through the slips down to third man. He charged up the wicket with his eyes on the fieldsman and crashed into me in my follow through. I thought he had done this intentionally, so I picked him off on the way back. He made his ground, then started advancing down the wicket menacing at me with his bat and making all sorts of threats. Graeme Watson had the ball and threatened to run Bedford out, so he scampered back to ground, leaving me furious about the whole affair. I was livid. I stormed back about 10 yards beyond my normal mark and streaked in at breakneck speed to let fly the fastest ball of my life. All my emotions went with that ball, but Bedford still got across behind it, even got his bat to it, but the ball just ploughed on relentlessly and crashed into his stumps. When we later discussed the event Peter assured me he hadn't even seen it, and I'm sure he didn't.

I was picked for the first international, to be played in Brisbane. That was a fairly inconclusive game all round. A total of 686 minutes were lost because of rain and when we did play it was a batsman's paradise. Only 15 wickets fell while 1002 runs were scored and they included five individual centuries, two of them to Ian Chappell. My return was a far-from-impressive 3-111 for the game. Then it was back to Perth for the second international. Australia batted first and the Rest of the World attack of Sobers, Tony Greig, Bob Cunis, Richard Hutton, Bishen Bedi and Intikhab Alam provided few fears for our batsmen as we hurried along to 349 in the day.

The next morning I woke up feeling terrible. I was so lethargic that it was a struggle to even get out of bed. I staggered down to the WACA Ground, still not feeling right but well aware that I'd better pull myself together because I needed a good performance to hold my place in the Australian side. If ever a man needed a quick tonic it was me. Well, the first ball of the day gave me just that. The wicket had sweated a bit under the covers overnight and was decidedy faster than it had been the day before. That delivery was almost a wide, but from the way it flew through I could tell it was going to be a fast wicket. The second ball to the little Indian, Sunil Gavaskar, 'took off' and grazed his chest on the way through to the 'keeper. The fourth ball touched the top of his glove as he fended off and Rod Marsh was throwing it to the heavens in a trice. From there on there was a steady flow of wickets and the Rest of the World were all out for a staggering 59 before the end of the first session of play. After bowling for only 90 minutes I was back in the dressing-room with the figures of 8-29 from 7.1 overs next to my name. It was almost unbelievable. After bowling four of those overs I recall saying to Ian Chappell that I didn't feel too good and wanted to have a spell. He said, 'See if you can bowl a couple more'. Nothing happened in the next over, but then things started to go haywire. Wickets fell and fell and the last six wickets came my way in the space of 15 balls without my conceding a run. Eight for 29 is a shade better than 2-29, which is roughly how things looked when I asked for a spell!

How did it happen? I guess the day was right for fast bowling and it was perhaps the fastest wicket I've ever bowled on. There was a good crowd who were right behind me and that gave me a lift. And, of course, there were some brilliant catches among those eight dismissals. It was just one of those freakish happenings in sport where everything seems to go right for an individual. Back in the dressing-room I just plonked down in my seat thinking 'thank goodness that's over, now I can have a spell'. It had been only 90 minutes, but I was absolutely exhausted. It was probably the toughest hour and a half I've ever spent at cricket. I have bowled many more than 7.1 overs on the run before in much less pleasant conditions and pulled up feeling far better than I did that day. I can only think it was because I had bowled every single ball of that spell flat out. The emotions and tensions would have taken their toll, too. Far from having a shower and putting my feet up for the rest of the day, I had to pick myself up and go again as Ian Chappell had decided to enforce the follow-on. It was too much for me. I recall muttering something inane like 'Does that mean we have to bowl again?' I didn't want to go out, I was a spent force. I bowled a couple of overs in the new innings and got the wicket of Farokh Engineer before lunch for a tally of nine victims for the session, but then I had to call it a day. I ended up with four wickets for the innings and a total of 12-92 for the game.

My success in that game gave me confidence, but had a steadying effect on me. My feeling was 'You've done that, now settle down to prove to yourself and the world that it wasn't a fluke'. I guess that was my best 'on-paper' performance, but I can't help feeling it just came right for me. I have derived far greater satisfaction from other less remarkable achievements, such as being a member of the squad who won the Sheffield Shield for WA that season. That was an overall team performance and I was proud to have played my part in it. Another more rewarding experience for me was to take 10 wickets in the Fifth Test against England at The Oval in 1972. That effort helped Australia square the series against England. It had been a gruelling sort of game and I had fought to take every one of those wickets. Compared with the ideal bowling conditions at the WACA Ground, the Oval Test was really hard work. I think that performance against the Rest of the World was just my day, everything went right, there were brilliant catches and there was a 'run' on.

If ever I was caught on the rebound it was in the third international, played on the Melbourne Cricket Ground a couple of weeks later. Gary Sobers was the man responsible. He had scored 20 not out and 15 not out in the Brisbane international and I had nailed him for a 'duck', caught at the wicket by Rod Marsh, in the first innings of the Perth game. In the second innings of the Perth match he collected 33 before falling to Graham McKenzie. When I had the 'master' caught at second slip by Keith Stackpole for another 'duck' in the first innings of the Melbourne clash I thought I was pretty clever. I was even looking forward to having another crack at him in the second dig. In my first over at the champion in the second innings I confidently fired in a bouncer, not always good policy in the third innings of a match on the MCG, but still . . . Sobers hooked it instinctively, didn't quite get onto the shot and the ball skied up behind square leg. Kerry O'Keeffe ran around from in front of square leg and just failed to make the catch.

That was the last sniff of joy for the Australian bowlers for some time. Sobers just took charge of the situation and took runs as he pleased, compiling a magnificent 254 which included two sixes, taken from successive O'Keeffe deliveries, and 35 fours. The innings was 376 minutes of glory. Sobers played almost every stroke you can imagine, and some the normal player wouldn't dare imagine! All our bowlers took their share of hammer. It was superbly-controlled aggression and there was nowhere, repeat nowhere, you could bowl to contain the man. One of the best deliveries I sent down to him, a yorker with the second new ball, came back past me as though it had been fired from a cannon. It had crashed into the fence under the sightboard before I had been able to falter in my run and look back over my shoulder. It was a slashing, crashing drive that I'll never forget. Sobers was dynamic. He often just stood his ground and, with a beautiful slashing motion, scornfully swiped the ball through the gaps to plough into the wrought-iron fence around the MCG. The gates were open and Sobers just bolted! I place the innings on a par with Richards's treble century against WA as the best innings I've ever seen. The innings was watched by Sir Donald Bradman, who paid it what must be the ultimate tribute with these words: 'I believe Gary Sobers's innings was probably the best ever seen in Australia. The people who saw Sobers have enjoyed one of the historic events of cricket. They were privileged to have such an experience.'

5

After my crisis in the next game against the Rest of the World in Sydney and the tedious period of convalescence I concentrated hard on running and building up my stamina as much as I could in preparation for the tour of England. I spent a lot of time training with the Perth Football Club at Lathlain Park at the invitation of Greg Brehaut, one of the best exponents of the game in Australia and a former cricketer with my club, Perth. The Perth Football Club presented me with an embroidered towel, bearing their best wishes for the tour. I still use that towel at every home first-class game and for all club games. So, when we took off for England I felt in the peak of condition and confident I would have no trouble with my back.

It was bitterly cold when we arrived in England in April 1972 and I wore three sweaters when I went to the nets for the first couple of weeks. I took great care to warm up properly before all our early sessions, doing a lot of exercises in the dressing-room first, then running three laps of the ground at Lord's to get the blood flowing before I went to the nets. I had a very light workout on the first day at Lord's and gradually built up the tempo over the next three days. On the fifth day I decided it was time to build up to something like full pace. I gradually took my run-up further and further back and everything was all right until I tried to let one go from my full run-up at almost full tilt. Immediately I felt pain in my back, shooting pains up the spine, just as I had suffered in Australia. That came as a great shock to me, because I had almost forgotten about my back troubles and had just given myself the same easy build-up that the other quickies on the team had been through. Of course I had a fleeting query in my mind about how things would go, because I hadn't bowled really fast for more than three months. But it was only a passing thought and this was by no means a new fitness test. I kept bowling for a few more deliveries, but it was hurting considerably, so I left the nets and went in to see the team masseur, Dave McErlane from Sydney. Dave had a look, gave me a rub-down and made me do a few exercises before having a hot bath and calling it a day.

I was up bright and early the next morning and round at Dave's hotel room doing some exercises with him. It seemed as though everything was all right again . . . maybe I had been imagining things. I did more exercises at the ground before going into the nets again, where I went through a very slow build-up. I started at slow-medium, gradually building up to the moment of truth — the moment when I put some pressure on my back. But as soon as I put on any pace my back hurt. Ian Chappell walked across to me to see how I was going. There were umpteen pressmen hanging about, all after the tiniest thread of a story, so we decided to try to hide it from them for the time being. I just moved away from the nets to do some fielding before having a workout with the bat in the nets. As I stood in a group doing some catching practice it suddenly hit me . . . here I was on my dream tour of England and it looked as though I mightn't even bowl a ball in anger. I felt extremely depressed, as though the world was caving in around me. Back to the masseur, who gave me a cheery 'You'll be okay, it's only the cold weather' as he rubbed my back and sent me to have a hot bath. The pain eased off again, but it was decided I should be taken to see a doctor.

Alun Thomas was a tall, thin and rather stately gentleman in his late 40s. He had black, curly, short-cropped hair, a very friendly face, with a rather nonchalant way about him and a wonderful dry sense of humour. He was always laughing and always making people around him smile. He seemed very interested in you and gave you great confidence in his ability. He would always listen to what you had to say and would then go into a huddle with himself before giving you a rather precise answer in his refined English voice. Indeed Alun Thomas was anything but the picture I had conjured up of a Harley Street specialist. He looked and acted more like an Aussie. I was pleasantly surprised at our first meeting in his surgery in Park Street, near Hyde Park. It was situated on the ground floor of a rather plain two-storey building. I never saw inside his consulting room because he always met me in the entrance hall and took me straight to a treatment room. It turns out that 'doc' was very keen on sports and we often saw him when we played in London. He would breeze into our rooms at afternoon tea and have a pleasant half-hour with the lads, the enjoyment of the whole situation being shared by everyone. On that cool day late in April warmth came into my life when a relationship began which was to have a big bearing on the outcome of the tour as far as I was concerned.

The Doc gave me a thorough examination, but at the end

offered no comment on what might have been wrong with me. 'We'll get you right,' he said. 'Don't worry, you'll be right.' He was sure that through one means or another he would get me right for the tour. This was great news because I was just beginning to wonder if the tour would ever get off the ground for me. I didn't attend practice the next day, which set the pressmen buzzing and the manager was forced to tell them that I'd felt a twinge in my back and been forced to go to a doctor. I wasn't picked for the opening one-day game at Arundel against the Duke of Norfolk's XI and remained in London for treatment twice a day. The first time I bowled was in a knock-up game between the touring party at The Oval when I sent down a couple of overs off a short run without any side-effects. My hopes were rising that the treatment was working and that I'd be all right. Our first real game was at Worcester and I went with the team, not to play but to get treatment from Dave McErlane (under instructions from the doctor). On the second day I went to the nets to give my back a trial. It was all right at medium-pace, but the pain came shooting back when I tried to go any faster. Dave later rang the doctor in London and reported back to me that it had been decided it was not muscular trouble, rather that it was joint trouble, causing inflammation. 'You can't do yourself any harm,' he reported to me. 'You've just got to go out and bowl and if it hurts a bit, just keep on bowling.'

I wasn't too happy with that idea, but I wasn't going to question a London specialist's advice. So I went back to the nets to do as I had been told. It was useless. The pain was so great that I had to quit and go back to the dressing-room. I couldn't face Dave again, so I went straight to the bathroom and started to run a bath. Keith Stackpole could sense I was most upset and he came in to ask me how I was. I was so emotional and so distressed that I just broke down and started sobbing like a child. I guess that was a silly thing to do, but I was so mixed up that I couldn't control myself. Stacky was tremendous. He stayed with me and consoled me. 'Don't worry pal,' he said, 'We're all behind you. It'll come good. You'll be right.' I'll never forget the way Stacky helped me through that crisis. He gave me that little bit of confidence I needed to keep me going without the fear that I might be sent home.

It appeared then that I would just have to learn to absorb the pain each time I bowled. I decided to give it a go. I shouldn't proceed without saying that Ian Chappell was also a great help during these tenuous times. He went out of his way to see me at least once a day to ask how I was going and he often organised meetings that also included Stacky (who was the tour vice-captain) and the team manager, Ray Steele. Ian knew what the doctor had said, of course, and he had a chat with me about my playing in the next game, against Lancashire, and it was decided I had to play to test the new theory. It was a very cold day at Old Trafford and I did plenty of loosening up before I bowled, but still I suffered from pain — even at half-pace. I tried to operate off my full run-up, but I was only working on one side and couldn't get any pace at all. I bowled eight overs and took one wicket — that of Clive Lloyd, who was beaten by the (lack of) pace and was caught off a skied shot whilst trying to hook a short one. It was when I was having a rub-down after the game that the thought struck me . . . the tour was over for me! I had failed the big test and I might as well call it a day.

I must have been terrible company in those bleak early days of the tour. I just moped around the hotel and had no zest for anything. The boys did their best to keep me humoured, but it must have been hard work to get even a smile out of me. The former Australian player, Jack Fingleton, was one of the journalists with the team and one night in Manchester he called me to his room in the hotel. He had seen the pathetic way I had bowled and could sense I was bitterly unhappy. He told me he had been through a lot of back trouble and suggested a few exercises I might try to help overcome the problem. He had a bit of a chat with me and that helped to cheer me up.

The next game was at Nottingham and I was picked to play again. I went to the nets the day before the game and still suffered whenever I tried to put any pressure on my back. But on the morning of the game I felt very different. Instead of tentatively getting out of bed, I sprung out and felt really good. In the nets before play I even dared to try a couple of pretty quick ones and got by without any pain at all. My hopes soared sky high and I ventured to really test my back out in the middle. Things went well for a while, then all of a sudden the sharp, shooting pain was there and I was downcast again. It was like being dumped by a wave in the surf . . . one minute you're riding high and the next you're underneath the whole weight of it. I bowled 12 overs and just finished the game out. That's it, I thought, it'll never come good. I had been having treatment after treatment — in fact, I began to feel more at home on the rub-down table than I did on my bed and the doctor's surgery was like an extension of my hotel room. Things were becoming desperate. The first Test at Old Trafford was less than a month off and I was getting nowhere. It was then that the doctor made a decision, one which he had spoken of as the last resort: he would manipulate my back in a last-ditch effort to get it right. We went back to London for the Surrey match. I was left out of the side and arrangements were made for the manipulation to be done under a general anaesthetic in Mr Thomas's treatment room and with the help of our masseur.

I went along with Dave one bright London morning, completely oblivious to what was about to happen to me. I was given the knockout drop by an anaesthetist and from then on for half an hour or so my body was put through a pretty thorough manipulation. I'm told almost every bone in my body was given treatment, but of course the action was centred on my spine. Dave claimed afterwards that he did all the manipulation, whilst the doctor supervised, thereby making him an expert on manipulation overnight. Apparently there were many minor creaks and cracks of the bones — and two loud crunches which Dave reckons really pleased the doctor. After it all I went back to the hotel and slept for the rest of the day and that night. I was given instructions to bowl, and bowl flat out, the next day, so off I trundled to The Oval, full of apprehensions and expectations.

I bowled before the game started and everything felt good until I built up to top pace, when the pain started to come back. The Doc had said keep at it, so I pressed on, but soon the pain was unbearable. I went back, more than somewhat dejected, to the dressing-room for a rub and a hot bath. At lunch time back I went to the nets with the same result, although I had built up quite considerable pace. The advent of the players on the field after the break saved me from further punishment. That was a break-through day for me, because although it had still hurt a lot, I had bowled pretty fast. I was up on cloud nine . . . or at least on the way there. I didn't return to the nets during that game, just did plenty of running in the streets around The Oval and lots of exercises.

Off we went to Southampton to play Hampshire and I nursed myself along in the opening spell against Barry Richards, building up a little pace, but suffering no pain at all. We could all sense things were on the improve, and I started to smile for the first time on the tour as my fears and apprehensions melted away with each ball. I bowled 16 overs and got a couple of wickets in the first innings and was really looking forward to the second innings. The wicket was fairly slow by then, but I built up some pace in the 15 overs I bowled. I took only one wicket, but I was really excited about the way things had gone. I felt the other players were pretty excited, too. They had been through it all with me, in a way, and it must have been a big release to them to see me sparking again. Through it all my roommate David Colley had been tremendous. He was having a little back trouble, too, and each morning we'd get each other up at 6 o'clock and dart round to the masseur's room to do exercises under his supervision, and with him hopping into it with us. Some of the boys may have had their doubts about me and my courage after they heard that the Doc had told me I couldn't do any harm and yet I still wasn't getting anywhere. If they did have any questions I wasn't aware of it at any stage. Their wonderful support obviously came from the great team spirit that Ian Chappell built right from the start of the tour. The bus trip back to London from Southampton was a night to remember for me. I was in such high spirits that I had a rare (for me) flirt with the booze. I had a few drinks and got pretty tipsy — though I fancy I was so elevated in spirit that I would have needed only to sniff the cork of a whisky bottle to get high!

The next hurdle was the MCC match at Lord's. It was our first confrontation with a representative side — our first real trial of the tour — and I was picked to lead the attack. I was very tense before play started, harbouring a feeling that 'this was it'. And it was. In the first over of the game I got a couple past Boycott's bat. They went away a little, but they really just beat him for pace. You couldn't imagine how elated I was as I pulled my sweater on and went to my position as Bob Massie took up the attack at the other end. Then in my second over I had Boycott lbw with a ball that did nothing through the air or off the wicket. It simply beat him for pace. This was seventh heaven for me. A wonderful feeling of freedom overcame me and I nearly wept, but this time for joy. The lads were just as happy as I was, probably because we could all sense that trouble was a thing of the past and now we could get down to the serious business of winning the Ashes.

That was the start of the tour for me. I had no more back troubles from then on, no matter how hard I worked. Each morning and night for the rest of the tour I had a hot bath and each day I did exercises and plenty of running — I knew I would need fitness to carry me through the next three and a half months. In retrospect, I guess I can thank our masseur, Dave McErlane, for all the work he did to help me recover. I can thank Stacky, Ian Chappell and Dave Colley for their special efforts to keep me going. I can thank the rest of the players, particularly the WA boys in the party, for the way they stuck with me. But the man I thank most is that rather suave, not-so-English gentleman Alun Thomas, who kept a watchful eye over me throughout the tour and whose masterstroke salvaged everything for me. The Doc later wrote and asked me if I would write a chapter for him in a book he was compiling. The subject was my training build-up for a new season and I derived a great sense of pleasure from writing that chapter and doing the Doc a small favour for all those he had done for me.

The First Test was at Old Trafford early in June and I was rarin' to go. England won the match by 89 runs late on the last day, but it is my firm belief that had Australia been able to play Bob Massie in this game a good performance by him could have turned the tide our way. It was a lively seamer's wicket and would have been right up Bob's alley. The NSW seamer Dave Colley played and took four wickets for the game. I am certain Bob would have lapped up the conditions and have done even better. John Snow, Geoff Arnold and Tony Greig cut our batsmen to ribbons with a professional performance in conditions they knew so well. A highlight of this game was a scintillating 91 by Rod Marsh in the second innings. It was a wonderful display by Rod, including four towering sixes off the lefthand orthodox spin of Norman Gifford. When he fell, after a stand of 104 with John Gleeson, some of us wondered if he was ever to get the Test century he so richly deserved. In 1971, at the Fifth Test against England in Melbourne, Bill Lawry had shocked the cricket world by declaring when Rod was 92 and 'looking at' his first Test 'ton'. Rod got his Test century the season after we arrived home, in the Adelaide Test against the Pakistanis.

I was reasonably happy with my eight wickets for the Old Trafford match, though I was fully aware that conditions had favoured my type of bowling. Hard work lay ahead, I was sure. Australia's hopes were dented, but not daunted, by that loss and we went to Lord's confident of levelling the score in the Second Test. This game will always be recalled as Massie's Match because it was in this Second Test, Bob's maiden Test at the age of 25, that he carved out a niche in cricket's history by taking 16 wickets for 137 runs. Bob bamboozled the England batsmen with an immaculate display of swing bowling. True, conditions were ideal for swing bowling, overcast and humid weather prevailed almost throughout the match, but Bob proved it was no fluke when he continued to swing the ball viciously in totally different conditions at Trent Bridge in the Third Test. It was a truly great performance. And through it all Bob remained the same old dry-as-chips Bob, trundling away to the best of his ability, just weaving a web around the English batsmen. I remember looking up at the scoreboard on one occasion during the second innings, when England were 5-31, and scratching my head in wonderment that it could be true. One thing that thrilled me about the final scoreboard was the fact that it was all Western Australia . . . Massie 16 wickets, the other four mine. Bob's was as near to perfect a piece of bowling as I could imagine. Throughout the long spells he bowled, he maintained a high standard of accuracy and penetration, something that I've only dreamt of as a bowler. The crowd, particularly the vocal cricket-lovers from the West Indian and Pakistani population in London, lapped it up. They cheered Bob each time he completed his over and returned to his spot at fine leg or third man down at their end of the ground. Such a performance gave us a wonderful lift.

The following night we attended a function at the National Sportsmen's Club and it turned out to be one of the most memorable nights of our lives and one which none of us would have missed it for anything. The company was exhilarating, we all sat next to notable British sportsmen and conversation didn't lapse from start to finish. Even though it started out as a formal evening, the food, the wine and the company was so agreeable that before long there was a most relaxed atmosphere surrounding us all. Impromptu questions were fired across the tables, impromptu answers were fired back and it was stimulating, to say the very least. But that function was just the kick-off. At midnight we were picked up and taken to a recording studio nearby, where we had the most hilarious time putting on wax the team's two songs, 'Here Come The Aussies' and 'Bowl A Ball, Swing A Bat'. The result of those hours of blood, sweat and tears in that recording studio was a record that sounded reasonably musical and indeed sold a fair few copies, although the story has it we didn't sell a single copy in Engand!

Salute modern technology, because not only were we a motley bunch of singers, but we were a very merry gathering throughout the whole operation. We were all rather looking forward to the experience, most of us fancying it would be just a matter of opening our mouths and out would come the magic of melody. But it was more than three hours before we were finally released from that studio, more than somewhat sobered by our experience and raspy of voice. And the technicians and people from the recording company told us it was one of the quickest recording sessions they had ever had! To us it had seemed like a lifetime of run-throughs and rejections. Somebody had organised a few dozen cans of beer, which kept the throats lubricated and David Colley kept us amused in between 'takes' with his parody of one of the employees of the recording company. 'Now come on sweeties, don't let's waste any time,' he would say in a high-pitched trill. 'Hold on to that note a bit longer, Stacky. Now don't you go too high, Beatle . . .' I think the technicians wondered what sort of a bunch we were. The whole team and all the officials were there for the session and I have my suspicions that the first 20 run-throughs were used to sort out the singing voices from the tone-deafs. There was a lot of shuffling of players from microphone to microphone. Then, when the men were sorted out from the boys some of the mikes were turned off, and I'm pretty sure I ended up on one of the dummy mikes! Doug Walters was quite funny. He fancies himself as a bit of a crooner and if you listen closely to the record, you will hear him lifting his voice at the odd time and making himself sound a bit different from the rest of the boys. It was a tremendous night from start to finish, one that will be with me always.

About 10 days later we met Leicestershire at Grace Road and one of the real pleasures for me was playing against Graham McKenzie, a West Australian who was then playing in the Leicestershire County side. He and I agreed that when he came in I would bowl him a high bouncer for the first ball which he would try to hook. It was a deliberate set-up. I put down a ball which went a mile high over Garth's head and he looked like one of the world's outstanding batsmen in trying to deal with it! The effect on the crowd was as we had anticipated and if their attention had been wandering, they were certainly concentrating now.

We settled back into the routine of the game, but three balls later as I was returning to the top of my run-up I noticed that a tennis ball had been hit onto the ground by a young lad playing cricket with his mates near the sightscreen. I stopped as casually as I could to pick it up, slipped the real ball in my back pocket and ran in to deliver my 'shock' ball. It frightened 10 months growth out of Garth and our wicketkeeper, Rod Marsh, and drew a couple of comments from my teammates that are worth repeating. Bob Massie, who was at the time fielding at fine leg, said he thought I'd bowled one so fast that the cover had come off the ball. John Inverarity, standing at first slip, commented immediately that he thought the delivery was so fast that the ball had turned white hot! The staggering thing about it was the fact that a person in the crowd had actually photographed the delivery and a picture of the tennis ball going by McKenzie was published in the English Press. It was all a good laugh then, but I must report that Garth had the last laugh on me. The occurrence was a double-wicket competition being held at the Floreat Park Cricket Club in Perth towards the end of the following Australian summer. Garth and I were paired against each other and the Grace Road ground at Leicester was far from my mind when I went in to face McKenzie and his partner, Ian Brayshaw. After a couple of sharpish deliveries with a cricket ball, Garth quietly switched to a tennis ball that he had hidden in his back pocket and let one fly at me. I almost fainted from the shock!

I guess the purists don't get much of a laugh from such things happening on the cricket field, but I believe there's nowhere near enough colour in our game. Within reason, these diversions can only help attract people to the game. I was at it again during the English tour when we played, or tried to play when the weather permitted, a game to celebrate the Centenary of the Sussex club at Hove. When we finally got a start, I decided it was time to liven things up so I took out a red apple in my pocket. I bowled a couple with the new ball, then made the switch and fired a quickie down with the apple. The Sussex batsman carefully played forward, but threw his head back in amazement when the 'ball' disintegrated before his eyes as it hit the pitch. I noticed that part of the apple had struck the batsman on the pads, pretty well in front, and that the rest of it had hit the stumps, but not knocked off the bails. That old Australian campaigner Bill Alley was umpiring at my end and as he muttered and spluttered about what was going on, I appealed for lbw and bowled. That snapped Bill out of his 'nightmare' and he avoided an international incident by calling it a 'no-ball'!

With any sort of luck we could have won the Third Test at Trent Bridge. But, after holding all the tricks and dictating terms for the five days we had to settle for an honourable draw on a wicket that can only be described as a featherbed. Again Bob Massie had sliced into the England batting, again he had successfully used tactics of bowling around the wicket in spells to throw the batsmen off their balance. This was a plan devised before the Lord's Test and how well it worked for the two matches. I fancy that after that the ultra-professional English batsmen managed to adapt their style to cope with such a change of line. It was a clever piece of strategy, though, and typical of the lengths a team must go to in its planning in Test cricket these days.

Then to the Fourth Test, the series still all tied. All I can say about this game is that it was one of the greatest disappointments in my cricket career. The way things turned out at Headingley put paid to any theories I may have had about 'honour among thieves'. We had been led to believe that the Headingley wicket would play as it had done throughout the early stages of that season — a seamer's paradise. I recall strolling across the ground to have a look at the strip on the day before the match. It was completely devoid of grass. We were still none the wiser. The strip may have looked brown while the rest of the square was lush green, but it normally seamed a bit and that was what we expected. We did get some inkling of what was to come when England suddenly brought Derek Underwood into the side and dropped Norman Gifford, who had played the first three Tests. But we had no idea of the nightmare that lay ahead of us. We batted first and it was soon quite obviously a diabolical 'turner'. Underwood and Illingworth were treacherous operators and they had our best batsmen groping throughout the two innings. Perhaps the only Australian innings of any substance was that of Paul Sheahan in the second innings. The tall Victorian kept his head down almost on the wicket to be unbeaten on 41 when the Australian innings closed. I suppose you could say we had our chances. We scored 146 and had England 7-128. Had we been able to clean up the home side's tail we could have made a game of it. But our spinners' fingers grew tired and a century stand by Illingworth and Snow broke our hearts.

I remember the feeling that went through my mind at the end of the first day's play. It was one of bitter disappointment, one of having been 'sold out'. The conditions so heavily favoured the home side as to make it not even a match. An enquiry later revealed it was some sort of fungus in the wicket which had caused the grass to die and make the strip turn so much. And possibly that was the cause of the situation. I thought the grass was cut down so bare that it was through to the roots. No matter what the cause it certainly was not a wicket of Test match standard. When a bowler of John Inverarity's modest talents can return figures of 33 overs, 19 maidens, three wickets for 26 runs against batsmen experienced in these conditions there ought to be a Royal Commission into the preparation of the wicket. True Invers is a handy bowler, but those are the figures of an out-and-out champion. I am told Trevor Bailey in his comments on the match on the BBC said the wicket was no more than a 'slow turner' and that any English county side would have had little difficulty in scoring 250 against the England spin attack. I agree that the wicket was generally slow, (though the odd delivery just 'took off') but the amount of turn derived even by Illingworth, who is not a prodigious turner of the ball, was staggering. And Underwood, who bowls at more like medium-pace, was still turning appreciably and of course was almost unplayable. Obviously the home country in any series isn't going to prepare wickets to suit the touring side. But at least they should prepare fair wickets of Test match standard. It's too far to travel to have to put up with sub-standard wickets without making some sort of protest. I agree the Englishmen must have their troubles in adapting to the fast wickets in Australia, but I would be ashamed to think such a poor wicket would be turned on for any touring side in Australia. Our attack had shown a liking for wickets that gave some help to the seamer, as we had found at Old Trafford, Lord's and, to a lesser extent, Trent Bridge. It was strange the way things changed at Headingley especially bearing in mind the way the wicket had played earlier on in the season.

The outcome of the series hinged on the Leeds Test and when the Ashes were safe after that game we found a very fair wicket at The Oval for the Fifth Test. From a fast bowler's point of view the Headingley wicket was just a waste of time. At no stage did I feel confident of taking a wicket. At no stage did I feel like anything more than a medium-pacer, and that's a depressing thought for a quickie. In the end I just bowled within myself and just hoped the batsman would make a mistake. The couple of time I tried to bowl a bouncer I was embarrassed by the result. It was just a joke. The Australian team's morale, so high after the fine win in the Second Test and our great effort at Trent Bridge, just caved in on the first day of the Leeds match. I don't think our boys recovered from their initial feeling of having been cheated.

The Fifth Test at The Oval was a wonderful climax to the series for Australia. After our body blow in the previous Test we became more determined to win this Test — and win it well. And that's what we did. The wicket gave a little encouragement to the seamers, a little to the spinners. This game gave me great personal satisfaction, because I toiled hard in bowling 56.4 overs and saw the rewards of my labours in the shape of ten wickets for the match. This took my total for the series to 31, a record for an Australian in England. All that after long periods of wondering whether I would ever bowl a ball in a Test match on the series! The game built up to a wonderful climax and when Sheahan and Rod Marsh steered us to victory with a partnership of 71 the scenes in the Australian dressing-room were amazing. We were all so thrilled to have taken our revenge on England and to have levelled the series. Our smiles were yards wide. Out on the field Paul and Rod whooped it up with a victory dance as they charged off to beat the engulfing crowd. There were real celebrations that night the details of which I'm not prepared to divulge!

The one-day series for the Prudential Trophy followed and this was a mistake as it should have been played in gaps between the Tests. I'm sure the players would have preferred that, so they could pack up and go home after the major Test series ended. It's far better that way. Any other games only prolong the agony of the wait to get home. But the games were good stuff, just what the action-hungry spectator of today wants. I think there is a place for this hit-and-run style of cricket, provided it is kept in perspective. It offers sure-fire action, a result in the day and the crowds love it. That means it brings in money for the game and who is going to knock that? I would like to see it developed to a situation where every couple of years there is a world one-day series, played in different countries on a rotating basis, televised to the other countries, a gathering of the world's best players all struggling for world championship honours. I have no fears for the future of Test cricket because of the growth of the one-day match. There will always be people who will go to watch the Tests. There is something completely different about a Test, there is a wonderful atmosphere and 'meaning' to the game at that highest of levels. So don't worry about Tests, they're here to stay. If one-day games have a fault it is the effect they can have on middle-order batsmen, often new young players, who need time to settle down. They are nearly always thrown to the wolves in the one-day game. That is why I say that this mini cricket must be kept in its right perspective.

I must admit that I was floundering for a goal in the first of the one-day Tests. I had 'spent' myself in the major Tests and I operated off a shortened run-up and consequently failed to take a wicket. I was even hooked a few times by Boycott who had regained sufficient fitness and composure to be included again in the England side. The English press thumbed its nose at me after that game with headings like 'Boycott wins war against Lillee'. That shook me out of my slumber and in the next game I was determined to show them just who was winning what war. I went back to my full run-up and knocked his middle stump out in the first over. That was one of the most satisfying moments in my cricket career. I also had Boycott caught on the hook in the third mini-Test. The Australians had put a lot of thought into Boycott before the tour opened. We had our plans and our counter-attacks all laid out because we saw him as the bogey-man and we were determined to see him off as soon as possible. I am not able to divulge these plans as they were aided in their formative stages by the observations of an Australian journalist, an ex-Test player who travelled with us. It was a successful plan and we may be able to use it again. Actually the series would be one Geoff would rather forget, I'm sure. His four Test innings, he missed the last three Tests through injury, were 8, 47, 11 and 6 and in the MCC versus Australia match at Lord's he scored only 2. In the one-day matches he scored 25, 8 and 14.

Over the whole English tour I bowled 456.5 overs in first-class games (249.5 of them in the Tests), and 33 more in the one-day series at the end. My tally for the tour was some 29 overs more than off-spinner Ashley Mallett, the next highest Australian in that tour.

6

As you can imagine I was a weary fellow when I returned to Perth at the end of the tour — and after four successive summers, two in Australia and two in England. After snatching a week's holiday with Helen I had to get back into training for the new season with Western Australia and the series against Pakistan, leading up to the tour of the West Indies the following February. Then began the onslaught — six tough games in as many weeks leading up to the First Test against Pakistan, then the three Tests in successive weeks. In all there were nine games in nine weeks, three of them five-day Tests. Here's how the Australian Cricket Board put me to work:

November 4-7, WA v NSW, in Perth: 34.7 overs, 3 maidens, 115 runs, 8 wickets.

November 18-21, WA v Pakistan, in Perth: 23.7 overs, 6 maidens 90 runs, 8 wickets.

November 24-27, WA v Qld, in Brisbane: 26 overs, 6 maidens, 71 runs, 5 wickets.

December 1-5, WA v NSW, in Sydney: 41.4 overs, 9 maidens, 147 runs, 9 wickets.

December 8-11, WA v Victoria, in Melbourne: 41 overs, 6 maidens, 172 runs, 6 wickets.

December 15-18, WA v SA, in Adelaide: 40 overs, 8 maidens, 147 runs, 8 wickets.

A total of 207.2 overs, 38 maidens, 778 runs, 44 wickets.

That number of overs was by far the highest number bowled by any Australian player to that date in the season — and that includes all the spinners. It may not sound much, but in the Australian summer it's plenty, believe me. In the Melbourne game I had to carry an extra burden because Bob Massie broke down. On a 'dead' Adelaide wicket I was called on to bowl more than I perhaps should have because we were very close to outright victory, but a lad called Trevor Chappell held us out. At the end of that game I was exhausted — yet I had to front up four days later for the First Test, also in Adelaide. As I hadn't been home for a month, I grabbed the opportunity to fly home with the WA team and spend a couple of days with Helen before returning for the Test. The Adelaide wicket was surprisingly lively on the first day and I picked up four wickets for my troubles. In the second innings it was pretty flat — and so was I. The hard work of the season so far was starting to tell on me. I could feel myself slipping. I had a pretty good rest before the Melbourne Second Test, then got a further respite when we batted first. I bowled reasonably well early in the piece, but I tired quickly and it was then that I started to get the feeling that perhaps things weren't right. At the time I wrote it off to the fact that I was just dog tired. Off we trudged to Sydney for the Third Test and I was dragging my feet at that stage. My figures for the first two Tests were:

First Test, in Adelaide: 35.3 overs, 10 maidens, 102 runs, 5 wickets.

Second Test, in Melbourne: 27.6 overs, 2 maidens, 149 runs, 3 wickets.

In the nets the day before the Test in Sydney I felt a slight twinge of pain in my back. I was bowling fairly well and didn't worry too much about it at that stage. When the game got under way the next day I was bowling fairly fast for a few overs. Then I came back for another spell, again building up some pace when suddenly my back just collapsed. I felt an enormous pain shoot right up my back. I couldn't fathom what was wrong, so I went straight off the field and was examined by Dr Corrigan immediately. Brian looked me in the eye and said: 'You've just had too much cricket. What you need is a long rest.' How right he was! He suggested that what was wrong with me was probably inflamed bone joints, or something like that, caused by overwork. He said I should have plenty of rest and some treatment by a physiotherapist and I should be all right for the West Indies tour. As I lay on the rub-down table in the dressing-room I had a visit from the Australian selectors, who didn't seem unduly worried. They told me to 'do what the doctor says' and not to worry. Then I had another visitor, Sir Donald Bradman, up from Adelaide for the Test. He stayed for some time and we had a very pleasant informal chat. We discussed the 1972 tour of England and he talked a bit about how drastically the mode of transport had changed since the early days of his tours to England. He advised me to rest up for the West Indies, then left.

The Pakistan innings ended, then Australia batted, then there was a rest day — and at the end of those few days of rest I felt pretty good within myself. Bob Massie and John Watkins put on 83 runs for the ninth wicket, leaving Australia with a fighting chance of snatching victory. I approached Ian Chappell and offered to bowl in a bid to help us win the game. If I broke down there was nothing lost, but perhaps I could help. Ian said all right, but it was up to me. The doctor gave his sanction, but warned me to take it easy. I got the masseur to rub some really hot liniment into my back, took a couple of painkilling tablets and went out for a crack at the Pakistanis. I bowled just just above medium pace and made the ball swing about enough to contain the batsmen at my end while Max Walker cleaned the tourists out with figures of 6-15 from 16 overs. I had bowled 23 overs and I came off the ground very sore and sorry for myself, despite our rousing victory. I went home to Perth with instructions to have more treatment in the 10 days or so we had before the team left for the West Indies.

Again I left Australia on a mission with an Australian team and again on reflection I'm not certain I should have gone with the touring party. I had simply reached saturation point after some two and a half years of high-tension cricket and I'm certain now that the right thing for me would have been to stay at home and rest, rest, rest. But at 23 I was still young enough have plenty of that crazy human ingredient called enthusiasm running through my veins. The thought of touring the Caribbean islands sent excitement down my wires and that spark of expectation put all thoughts of the consequences behind the door for the time being. So, for better or for worse, I arrived in Jamaica with the Australian party late in January — ready to take on the world!

The pain and anguish I had suffered the last time I had tried to bowl fast, in Sydney, was now only a fading memory. I was living for tomorrow — but tomorrow never came. In early practice at Sabina Park, Kingston, things went without incident. Oh, there were a few aches and pains, but you expect those if you haven't bowled for a while. I missed the one-day opening game against the University of the West Indies, but fronted up for the game against Jamaica. I operated off my long run-up and was reasonably happy with things, having built up a fair whack of pace. Again, a few aches, but nothing to worry about. I missed the next match, against the President's XI at Montego Bay, but was doing plenty of running along the beaches and the streets to keep myself as fit as possible. Then it was back to Kingston for the First Test. It was a fairly unresponsive wicket, but I was happy to have built up to a lively pace. I bowled 32 overs for the game and, though I didn't take a wicket, I had passed through it without taking any harm either.

It was in Kingston that Newcastle leg-spinner, John Watkins, was on the receiving end of one of Doug Walters many card tricks. John was no star with card games, but Doug was determined to teach him how to play 'switch', a fairly simple game which cricketers all over the world play to pass the time away in the dressing-room or on long flights. One night in Kingston a group of players left the pair of them in their hotel room while we went out for a meal. 'Wok'll know the ropes by the time you all get back,' Doug shouted as we left the room. We returned about three hours later to be told rather excitedly by Doug that Wok did indeed 'know the ropes'. In fact, said Doug, he was now quite a dab hand at switch. 'Look at this,' said Doug, as he dealt out a hand for the pair of them. The ensuing 'hand' was almost too much for the rest of us — Doug broke every rule along the way to winning the hand. Poor old John didn't have a clue he was being diddled. Then Doug showed us the scorecard. They had played umpteen hands in our absence and John had lost *every* one — he was trailing something like 3000 points to nil! Doug also is extremely clever at magician-type card tricks and nobody is ever too keen to play cards with him for money. With Doug I think cards is a medicine. A quick hand of patience if he has no takers for a game helps to soothe his nerves before going out to play.

We moved on to Antigua for the match against the Leeward Islands. I bowled a few fast overs, then tried for a little bit more in my second spell — and then my back just collapsed. Both sides were almost killing me with pain. I recall saying to Ian Chappell 'I think my back is broken', because I had no power in my back at all. I had no idea at all that indeed I *had* three breaks in my back, and it was a touch of irony that my first comment should be 'I think my back is broken'. Another touch of irony was that it was the last over of the day and Ian had asked me before the over if I wanted to 'have another go'. I had jumped at the chance. Had I not done so, who knows what the rest of the tour would have meant to me?

As it was, that was also the last over I bowled on that tour. There was always hope that there would be another Alun Thomas to wave his magic wand and bring me back into the side before the series ended. But, apart from a glimmer kindled by a radiologist called Rudi Webster in Bridgetown, Barbaros, the remainder of the tour was nothing more than a shuffle from one specialist to another — a constant flow of different diagnoses and a gradual dousing of the flame within me.

Rudi Webster had played first-class cricket in the West Indies and England, and I had met him when he was in Australia a few years earlier. He moved around the country, but worked at the Royal Perth Hospital for some time. He was a tall, loose-limbed fast bowler and I had met him at the WACA Ground, where he was attending State practice sessions by invitation. He knew most of the members of the Australian team in the West Indies, so it was no surprise to see him in Bridgetown. During a discussion I had with him he asked me about my back and said he thought he might be able to help me. He said he had been hit by back trouble when he was in England playing for Warwickshire and he fancied I may have the same trouble — stress fractures of the spine. At that time I was being treated by a specialist in Bridgetown and Rudi was reluctant to intrude on another specialist's business. The specialist was treating me for muscular trouble, but without any success. Then he manipulated my back, but again to no avail. So it was then that I decided to 'front' the team manager, Bill Jacobs, and ask his permission to consult Rudi, who just wanted to take a series of X-ray examinations to find out if indeed his theory was correct.

Permission was granted, so off I trotted to the hospital in Bridgetown for a long series of X-rays under Rudi's guidance. Many pictures were taken at all sorts of angles. After each sitting Rudi would examine the X-rays and then try a different angle. At that stage the West Indian all-rounder Bernard Julien was in the same hospital having X-rays taken of an arm that had been injured in the practice sessions leading up to the Second Test. Rudi's sittings lasted about two hours and entailed a great variety of positions and depths of bone layer in the photographs. Finally Rudi came into the waiting-room with a picture in his hand and pointed out three tiny fractures on two of my lumbar vertebrae. Rudi suggested a course of exercises he had used successfully to strengthen the stomach and back muscles enough to take the strain off the back. It was a wild shot in the dark, but now that I knew what the trouble was I was right in the mood for shots in the dark. So I dived into these exercises like a man possessed. Three times a day I tortured my body with as much work as it could stand. In between times I'd be off on a long run, to keep my legs and wind right so that if my back could stand it I would be fit enough to come back into the game later in the tour. My hopes started to run high and the exercises didn't hurt that much, perhaps because I could see something at the other end. There was light at the end of the tunnel at last.

One cheerful thing about being in Barbados was an extremely funny night with Wes Hall, in a three-hour, non-stop side-splitting session in a hotel room. Apart from having an unbelievable repertoire of jokes and stories about cricket and cricketers, Wes just has to be the most enthusiastic performer on cricket's funny stage. His ebony skin shines, his dark eyes sparkle and his pearly teeth glisten as his athletic body darts about the room giving illustration aplenty to the story at hand. I was lucky enough, and I count it as a real stroke of fortune, to have been one of five Australians present at the Wes Hall Show that night. He hardly took a breath between each joke and story. It was a truly wonderful experience and one I'll never forget. If Wes ever wanted to try out a career as a walk-up comedian, I'd give plenty to be his promoter!

Then I ran into trouble with other doctors in the Caribbean. By this time we had moved on to Trinidad and the team manager insisted that I go to see a specialist there. I had left the X-ray pictures with Rudi in Bridgetown and, no matter how hard I tried, I could not convince the specialist in Port of Spain that X-rays had revealed some fractures. He was convinced it was muscular trouble, and that was that! I'm told there are dreadful inter-island jealousies in the West Indies and in retrospect I feel I might have been caught up in something akin to that. I finally talked the specialist into taking some X-rays, but he had some measure of satisfaction in reporting that they had showed nothing at all. But he didn't have Rudi's knowledge of the fractures and the positions which laid them bare to an X-ray picture. The doctor was so emphatic that his diagnosis was correct that he wouldn't even allow me to have Rudi's pictures sent from Bridgetown. It was too ridiculous for words. Here I was, desperately trying to cling to a strand of truth and nobody seemed prepared to believe me. The doctor then suggested all I needed was a painkiller, but that failed dismally when I tried to bowl fast in the nets. I then got his attention for long enough to tell him what had happened when I was being treated by Alun Thomas in England. I gave him a detailed account, including the manipulation under general anaesthetic, and the specialist decided to give this a try. So I went into hospital for another pounding under the anaesthetic. Two days later I went to the nets and did my very best to bowl fast, but it was hopeless. By this time three Tests had passed, so the best I could do was keep on running and hope for some sort of a miracle to bring me around in time for the final Test, back in Port of Spain. But that was a slender, slender chance.

The tour started to become a nightmare for me. I had been through the mill a bit with injuries in the last couple of years and was fairly well buffered against the mental torment of it all. But it was starting to 'get at' me. I was sorely frustrated, watching my teammates run around and do all the things I longed to be able to do. But I was continually plagued by my aching back and this didn't help matters. Any movement that required sharp sideways twisting was sheer agony. One of the contributing factors in my emotional strain happened before the second Test in Bridgetown, when I was summond before a meeting of the tour executive. I was given an ultimatum that if I didn't make it for that Test they would investigate the possibility of having a replacement flown to the West Indies and sending me home. That threat, which also received some publicity in the Press, hung over me for some time before I realised there was no chance of the Australian authorities carrying it out. It was something to do with finance and the arrangements with the West Indies officials concerning the extra cost of fares for replacements.

Towards the end of the tour the idea was thrown around among the tour executive that I might be flown home via London, where I would consult Alun Thomas again and see if there was anything he could do to help. But Dr Thomas, who had done so much to see me through the English tour, was aware of the discovery of the stress fractures and told Pressmen in England that in the light of the breaks there was little he could do to help this time. Our thoughts ended there. So I finished the tour on a rather sour note, happy to return to Perth and put the experience behind me.

But it wasn't the end of my hardship. Then began the rehabilitation. I went to my orthopaedic surgeon who viewed the X-rays, checked on the offending area and encased me in a plaster cast from my buttocks to the top of my chest. I had to do everything with a ramrod-straight back, but it did what it set out to do — give my back a complete rest. It was extremely uncomfortable and the only respite I got was when I was standing up straight, but I couldn't stand up all day and all night! Lying down was always done with difficulty and, for maximum comfort, flat out on my back. Washing was my greatest bugbear. I couldn't allow the plaster to get wet so I had to have plenty of help from Helen each time I went through the tricky operation of washing myself. She helped sponge me as I kneeled in a shallow bath. Then she would have to help me get dressed. She was almost my servant for the six weeks I suffered with that plaster cast. I think Helen realised what I was going through and was prepared to do all she could to help pass the time away with as little discomfort as possible. She was really wonderful. I had trouble finding clothes that would fit. I had only one pair of trousers that would go around my extra-wide girth and I almost wore them out during those six weeks. There were times when I just had to have a change and then, rather than going out and buying another pair that would soon be useless I cheated by taking one of my own pairs and doing up the zip as far as I could and fastening the top with a safety pin. I had to wear a sweater all the time to cover up the plaster and this caused a few problems at the bank, because they had a rule barring employees from wearing sweaters. But they bent the rule when they realised the problem that confronted me.

I started asking myself a lot of questions at that stage. I asked myself if this was what you got for putting everything into your game? Would I ever play top-class cricket again? I realised the plaster cast was the best thing for me. I just had to put up with it if I wanted to regain fitness. I simply had to wait it out. Of course I was frustrated by it all, but I could put up with frustrations because I could see light at the other end of the tunnel.

Imagine my relief when the doctor hacked that plaster away from me! Then, to my horror, he considered putting on another cast, just to be sure. We struck a compromise and for the next couple of months I was restricted far less, but supported as much, by a specially constructed back brace. The key pieces of this monstrosity were aluminium bars moulded to the shape of my back and covered with padding and held firmly in place with webbing straps. The brace was more uncomfortable because to be effective it had to be very firmly attached. I had to pull the webbing straps really tight and at certain angles the aluminium bars dug into my back. But I had a little more movement and enjoyed the relief of being able to take it off to have a bath and before going to bed. Although I hadn't had any tests on my back by this time it was feeling a lot better.

The time wore on and in the last two weeks of the six-week spell with the brace I was really fed up with it. There were many times when I felt like ripping it off and burning the confounded thing. I'm sure that if the doctor had asked me to leave it on a day longer than the allotted time I would have done something drastic. To be finally rid of it was a wonderful feeling even though I was under strict instructions not to move sharply in case I undid all the good I had done. This period of cautious movement lasted about three weeks until I regained some strength in my back and midriff. Then the doctor gave me permission to start light exercise, stretching, flexing and some running. It was great to be back in action.

I kept buoying up my hopes of being able to play the following season and whenever I was asked the question, and indeed I was asked it a thousand times, I always replied that it wasn't too bad and I'd have to wait and see. I couldn't quite bring myself to admit that I wasn't going to play. I needed hope of some kind. Then one night John Inverarity telephoned me at home and wasted no time in getting to the point of his call. But this time it was different. Somewhat to my own surprise I said, 'It's no good, I'm not going to bowl this summer.' And that was that.

On my return from the West Indies I had taken up a partnership in a contract cleaning business and I was at it 13 hours a day with my partner to establish the business on a sound footing. I could see my hopes in business taking a hiding if I decided to put my energies into a first-class cricket season. I could also see that season being a disappointment as I wasn't putting enough time into my game because of the business, and when you are making a comeback after an injury you need to put in twice the amount of time you normally would to make sure you are in absolutely peak condition the whole time. Then there was Helen. I hadn't seen much of her in the past couple of years and she was pregnant for the first time. Further I realised that if I came back too early and failed I would inevitably lose my place in the Australian side and that would mean I wouldn't be in the team to play England during their tour of Australia in 1974-5. The decision was there all the time, but I just hadn't realised it.

How meaningless the summer was going to be! But how wrong I was. Because I can look back on the summer of 1973-4 and say honestly that it has been one of the most valuable seasons of my career. Without all the pressures of competition at the top I was able to devote myself almost entirely to developing technique, and learning a lot about the finer points of the game. A stroke of luck came not long after my big decision was made public when the Perth Cricket Club appointed me Captain-Coach.

The new element for me was that I was captain of the side, a position I had never experienced before. I found it embarrassing in the beginning, especially when setting fields in front of Rod Marsh, Mushtaq Mohammad and Gordon Becker, all men of far greater experience than myself. But I learnt from my mistakes and as the season progressed I gained confidence and I feel that I now know enough about captaincy to lead a team in a first-class match. That was a giant stride forward for me. Trying to make it again as a batsman was an equally imposing task. It had been many seasons since I had concentrated on this part of my game and I was very rusty. But, with plenty of advice, a lot of hard work and my share of luck I ended up having a fairly good season with the bat. I had to go right back to the basics of batting and that will never do me any harm. As time passed by my confidence grew, my defence became tighter and my strokes started to blossom. I scored 654 runs from 18 innings at an average of 43.6 and with a top score of 98. I learnt so much from that experience of batting with responsibility that I would gladly attempt to fill a higher spot than my customary 10 or 11 in the order for Western Australia and Australia. Then I saw marked improvement in my fielding. I was the captain, I had to set a good example, so I worked hard on my fielding and saw the rewards.

From the outset I stuck firmly to my decision not to bowl one ball in the nets or a match. I knew it wasn't going to be easy. Toiling in the field has been so much a part of me and standing back and watching others do it all was a strange experience indeed. As the games went by the frustration grew until it was almost unbearable. The pressure within myself was so strong that one day I rang my doctor just to discuss it with him, perhaps hoping that he would again firmly tell me not to bowl for fear of damaging the back again.

But, to my surprise, the doctor had weakened. He gave the nod of approval. He stipulated that I should go no faster than medium pace, work in short spells and stop immediately I felt any sort of pain. For the next couple of days I chewed it over in my mind — and still decided not to break my promise to myself. I would not bowl. But Perth were having their ups and downs and I felt if only I could have bowled a few overs here and there I might have been able to swing the odd game. We had three useful seamers in Ian King, Rod Gorey and Graeme Taylor plugging away, and here I was setting the fields for them and galloping around the paddock myself. It wasn't my idea of a cricket season. It was really eating me up, not being able to grab that ball and send a few down. The following weekend Perth were playing in a knockout game — against Melville — and I really wanted us to win that one, because I fancied we had a big chance to take the title. There was prestige and money (for the club) attached to it. We had made a dismal effort when we batted and the

South Australian opener Jeff Hammond plays a lofted drive for four runs at the WACA Ground

The next ball

A victory dance after having Mike Smith caught behind the wicket in the second innings of the First Test at Old Trafford

Dennis Lillee sends Geoff Boycott's cap flying with the first ball of the MCC's first innings against WA at Perth during their 1970-71 tour

Geoff Boycott again, bowled in the Second Test at Lord's

'You beauty . . .!' Whooping it up after the victory over England in the Second Test at Lord's. From left: Rod Marsh, Bob Massie, manager Ray Steele, Dennis Lillee, Ross Edwards, Ashley Mallet (back to camera) and Jeff Hammond

Dennis Lillee with his wife, Helen, and his mother

A lighter moment on the Australian tour of the West Indies. The great West Indian, Wes Hall, is the centrepiece in this impromptu steel band during a cruise off Barbados. With him are Dennis Lillee, Bob Massie, and Jeff Hammond

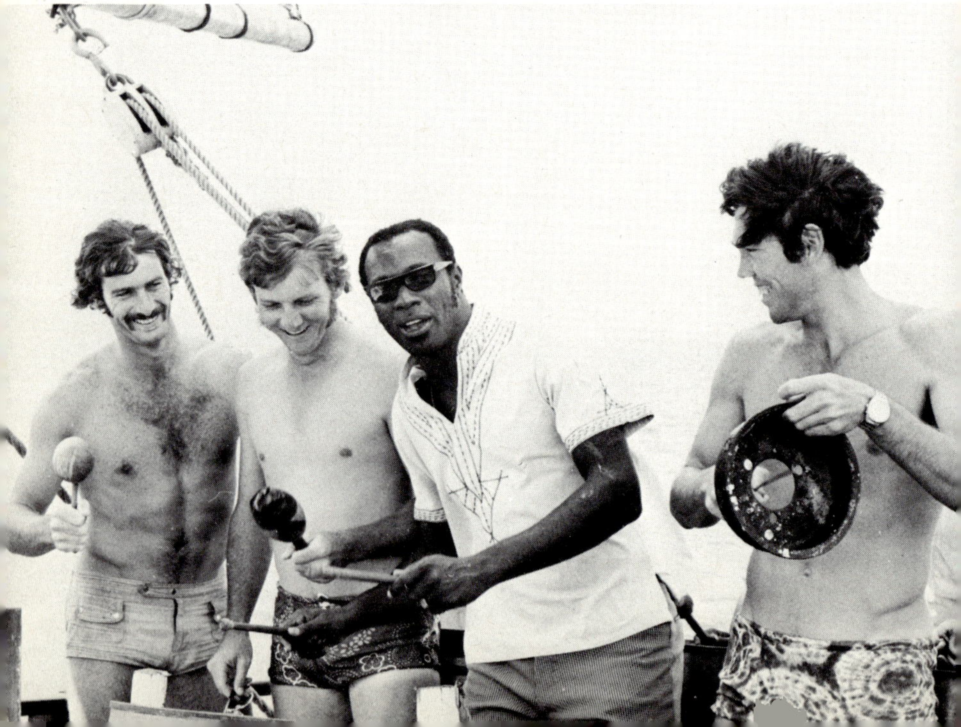

Landing at Perth after the Australian tour of the Caribbean. From left: Bob Massie, Ross Edwards, Dennis Lillee and Rod Marsh

A portrait of Gary Sobers by the famous Australian artist, Owen Garde (reproduced by permission of D. J. Tobin)

An unorthodox stroke at Floreat Park Cricket Club, Perth, against a tennis ball bowled by Graham McKenzie in retaliation against a similar delivery by Dennis Lillee in the Australia v. Leicestershire match the previous year!

On the way to the crease during a charity game at the WACA Ground in Perth!

'raining in the rain at
ıe WACA Ground
ɔr the 1972 tour of
ngland

In the shallows of the Swan River with Mal Brown and members of the East Perth Football Club before going to the West Indies in 1973.

And . . .

. . . training in earnest

Preparing for the 1974-75 season. Dennis Lillee works on a back exercise with Dr Frank Pyke at the University of WA

boys were bowling pretty poorly. The game was slipping away and my heart started to pound so hard that I was sure the lads could have heard it. Would I . . . should I . . . what? The next thing I knew I had the ball in my hand and was walking back five or six paces. The lads weren't sure what was going on. They waited for me to throw the ball to somebody. I was looking blankly ahead, still not sure whether or not I should go ahead with it. Then I shook myself and regained control of the situation long enough to start my first over for a long, long time. I hadn't even rolled my arm over in the nets, yet the first ball was bang on line, just a little short of a length. The feeling was exhilarating, as I knew it would be. After all that time, all those frustrations, the decisions, the agony . . . it all came flooding back and I was like a kid with a new toy.

I didn't bowl long that afternoon, it was no great test for my back because I built up no pace. But the fact that I suffered no after-effects from it, other than the usual aches and pains and stiffnesses you get after the first bowl for a long time, gave me great confidence that my back was right again. I knew I could find line and length again, but my back just *had* to stand up. It was something to build on, gradually, until I could look at myself and say, 'you're ready to fire again'. I bowled only occasionally for a few weeks. I had served my own purpose, I had proved to myself that I could bowl — now was the time to take the reins again and ease myself into it. The next time I bowled was a couple of weeks later, and again it happened by chance. I wanted somebody to bowl one over so I could change ends with the two men operating at the time. Before I realised it fully, I was on my way back and preparing to bowl the over myself. The will to bowl was too strong. That was before Christmas. After the New Year I bowled more and more, though I still took things steadily, operating in short spells, when and where I wanted. It was a blessing I was captain! I built up pace towards the end of the season and in the finals of the competition on the sharp WACA Ground wickets I was bowling near my top pace again. In my eagerness for the side to do well I may have bowled a little too much in the final, which we lost. It would have been Perth's first senior premiership and I wanted so badly to be the successful skipper. I bowled and bowled, got my share of wickets and built up a lively pace. I didn't ever return to my full run-up and I always felt strong within myself. That was a wonderful reassurance to me.

When the season ended I had 48 wickets at an average of 15.8, and I was well satisfied with things. I would like to have been able to say I was strong enough to stand by my decision, but I think it was a good thing for me that I didn't. At least I had bowled, at least I had found out that my back was fully healed, my form and pace had been encouraging, and I was all keyed up about the prospects of the following season. Apart from that I had learnt a lot about the art of bowling. While I was puddling along off my short run-up I worked on different deliveries, the in-swinger, two varieties of slower balls and cutters off the wicket. I worked at varying my pace and changing my delivery point at the crease for further variety. I couldn't pace blast the batsmen out, so I had to concentrate on line and length which was a good lesson — and I learnt the importance of bowling to your field. When you set your own field you learn that very quickly. I think I made very real progress on the technical side of my bowling, so much so that I reckon if I had to I could make a go of it bowling medium pace and just above at the first-class level.

7

To be successful a cricketer must have a burning ambition, a deep-seated and fervent desire to do well. Without this hunger for success you'll have more bad days than good ones, and you'll accept those bad days as 'one of those things'. If you are bitten by the success bug it will drive you on and you won't accept anything else. Of course, success is a long term thing. It is the achievement of a goal through a progression of minor successes. In cricket it will be runs and wickets that tell the story in the long run, but there will be days when you'll come off the field without great figures next to your name, yet be wholly satisfied that you've done your very best with what was offering. For example, a batsman may quite easily regard a score of 45 made in difficult conditions against a top-line attack to be an innings of far greater value than one of 200 he made in perfect batting conditions against an attack lacking penetration.

I can truthfully say I have never gone into a game of cricket without some sort of goal. Even in some of the minor games during the long and sometimes arduous tour of England in 1972 I was still stimulated by the need to work out conscientiously to keep my form up for the Tests. Without a goal in a game you are lost. I try to set myself a target, often one that may be out of my reach, each time I play a game. It is a conscious act and one I recommend to all sportsmen. Goal-setting and goal realisation goes back to your period of pre-season preparation. When you are running and training so hard that it is hurting, you can absorb a bit of that pain by telling yourself: 'I am doing this because I want to reach peak fitness for the coming season, so I can bowl, bat and field to the best of my ability and win a place in the State side and the Test side and, above all, do well.' You've got a distinct goal — it is imprinted on your mind, and it *does* take away some of the pain, which can be agonising at times, because to reach a high level of fitness you must train at top pace and attack the 'pain barrier' every time out.

Your aim is to be so fit that you are *never* found wanting through your physical condition in a game, no matter what the conditions or what your captain demands of you. I don't think anybody could ever achieve such fitness, but it gives you a good target to shoot at. Each training session I set myself a goal before I start — it might be eight circuits of the ground or park I have chosen — and I always push myself a little bit further. The next time out I set myself a target a little bit harder, and still go that extra yard before I give it away. To bowl fast off a long run-up you have to be extremely fit. It is vitally important to realise this and to condition your body accordingly. That goes for every cricketer. Obviously a spinner shouldn't need to be as fit as a quickie, nor should a batsman, but neither should neglect the need for good condition. For after all it's usually the tired shot that gets a batsman out. Had he been that little bit fitter he might have made a better job of playing the stroke and survived to add to his score, and his team's total. From what I can gather this fanaticism for physical fitness that is so much a part of Australian cricket these days is only a recent development. If that is so, I can only say I'd hate to have been a fast bowler in those olden days. I find it hard enough bowling fast when I'm reasonably fit, let alone trying it on without enough preparation.

Take batsmen, for example. The first half-hour or so of an innings requires enormous concentration because the conditions are strange and the bowlers at their peak of effort to dislodge the new batsman. But to be able to go on from there condition is needed. Batting is such a fiddly art. Just one lapse in concentration and it can be all over for you for the day. I've heard batsmen say they don't need to bother about training because they'll bat themselves into condition. That's false thinking, because to do that you would need a string of very long innings, and how do you last for a string of long innings if you are always getting tired and making errors? Also there's the situation of the opening batsman who puts in a really tough day in the field, then must pad up and keep out the new ball in fading light for the last 20 minutes of play. He must be really fit to keep his wits about him or he will be back in the pavilion before stumps.

As I said, a fast bowler needs more than anybody in the way of fitness and stamina because he is the one who does the hard work. He has to pound through that long run-up, thump his feet into the rock-hard turf and let the ball fly at speed all day, no matter what the temperature. His feet take a dreadful pounding, his ankles get sore, his shins ache and all his muscles groan and grumble, but he has to be able to respond to his captain's call for another fling in the last half-hour of play. You have to be able to answer any reasonable request from a captain. If you don't your form will suffer and so will your results.

My pre-season work usually starts about three months before the first game. I kick off with light jogging and body exercises, not too much, just enough to loosen up for a week or two. Then I build up gradually with the work-load, training consistently four or five nights a week, which I find more effective than two really hard nights, until near the start of the season I run four to five miles a night with the last two to three miles at a lively pace. Then I finish off with some of my own brand of sprints, simulating an exaggerated bowling run-up of about 70 yards, starting slowly like a fast bowler on his approach to the wicket and building up to a crescendo at an imaginary crease. Those wind sprints get me into a routine that's pretty hard to beat and they make me right at home when it comes to the big wind sprint of a lightning-fast delivery in a match. I also concentrate on body tone, without overdoing it with heavy exercises that may dull sharpness of movement. I do exercises that work over most muscles of the body, with plenty of emphasis on the stomach and back area. Perhaps the most important facet of stamina is the conditioning of the stomach muscles. They must be really taut and you must be prepared to do plenty of exercises in this area. It can be a painful experience, believe me. I am not very keen on weight training, because it can put on bulk and slow you down. But training is a very personal thing. You should consult an expert to work out your own training programme and work at it until you feel you have achieved the level of fitness you desire and need. If you are working out your own training routine, bear in mind the thought that conditioning must be designed to help body co-ordination, not to hinder it.

My advice to a young cricketer would be to always have

in the back of his mind a long-term goal — to represent his country for instance, which should be every young cricketer's aim — and to keep in the front of his mind a series of intermediate goals. Depending on your age and current level of achievement those goals could be to play for your school team, the local juniors, district first-grade, for the State and then for the country. As each one of these goals is superseded it *must* be replaced with another a little further away. You must never be satisfied with having reached one of your goals and then sitting back on your laurels. That's when your progress will come to a halt. When I first started playing cricket I set myself the long-term goal to play for Western Australia. I don't think I ever believed I could do it, but there it was. That was my goal and it kept me going. When I was first picked for WA I allowed the thought to pass my mind: 'I wish one day I could be chosen for a World XI.' But I soon squashed that one, because I realised it was too far away. I settled for shorter term goals like playing well for WA and then perhaps being chosen for Australia.

In an individual game I set myself to get rid of the first three or four batsmen before I take my sweater for my first couple of spells. That's how I look on my job with the new-ball, and I'm really disappointed with myself if I fail to make it. Failure makes me doubly determined the next time I'm given the ball in that innings. If I do succeed in my first goal, then I reckon any more wickets I get are cream on top of the cake. Your attitude to your opponent, whether you are a batsman or a bowler, is of vital importance. You have to steel yourself and whip up within yourself a feeling bordering on hatred for your opponents before you can really succeed at the highest levels. There can be no accepting second best. You aim for the top and to achieve it you must believe that you are top dog all the time. So there is no room for soft feelings towards your opponents, no sympathies, no hopes that they come through all right. When I am bowling my heart out the batsman at the other end has no face. Batsmen are like thieves to me, desperately trying to steal from me the ascendancy I believe is mine. And I treat them like faceless, meaningless thieves. I desperately want to get them out and it's amazing how often it works. The man who wants to succeed in a confrontation between batsman and bowler normally wins the day. If you are a bowler you must strive for complete control over the situation. I try to adopt a positive attitude and believe that the faceless batsman at the other end of the wicket is really worried about what I'm going to do next, rather than me worrying about whether he is going to take my bowling apart. I think I've rubbed up some batsmen the wrong way through this attitude, but I believe in winning at all costs and that's the way I play. Sometimes an opposing batsman will try to strike up a conversation with me out on the field, but I don't want to talk to him for one second. All I want is to see him off as soon as possible. There's plenty of time for pleasantries after stumps are drawn, and I'll always bury the hatchet and dive into a good conversation with an opposing player in those circumstances. That is one part of cricket that I live for, meeting people and striking up of friendships through the common bond of cricket. But when I am bowling I try to go the opposite way and find something about the faceless batsman that really annoys me, then I build on that until it becomes a sort of hatred that burns in my guts until I get him out. That feeling is explanation in some way for sudden outbursts I sometimes make to players after I've finally blasted them out. I'm just so pent up against the batsmen that I let him have a bit of my tongue as he goes. I realise that cricket can probably get on all right without such outbursts, but when there is a fire burning within you, you don't stop to think before saying and doing things.

And I believe that fire has helped in no small way to achieve my successes in cricket.

Part of a fast bowler's aggression can be expressed in bowling bouncers. When confronted with the question of what they are trying to do when they bowl a bouncer, most fast bowlers are reluctant to come out with an honest answer. A lot will say they hope to shake a batsman's confidence by making the ball fly near him, then possibly get his wicket through an indecisive stroke. That wears a bit thin with me. Why can't fast bowlers be honest and say: 'I bowl bouncers for one reason and that is to hit the batsman and thus intimidate him.' I try to hit a batsman in the rib-cage when I bowl a purposeful bouncer, and I want it to hurt so much that the batsman doesn't want to face me any more. I want to be in complete control of the situation and that's one way of keeping hold of the reins. I don't want to hit a batsman on the head because I appreciate what damage that can do. There can be nothing more deflating for a bowler, and inflating for a batsman, than a half-hearted bouncer and a batsman laughing at it as it goes harmlessly over his head. When I bowl a bouncer I try to make it a really good one every time. There's no point in bowling a weak bouncer because I'll lose ground, and that's the last thing I want. I appreciate from batting myself just how disconcerting a good bouncer can be. If somebody bowls one with plenty of venom that strikes me or just whizzes by my ear, then I'll certainly have second thoughts about that bowler from then on. I think most batsmen are the same. When I'm running in to bowl a bouncer I'm telling myself the whole way in: 'This has got to be fast, and I mean *bloody* fast, and it's got to land exactly where I want it.' Not many batsmen recover from a really good bouncer.

I have the attitude when I'm bowling that it is my right as a bowler to take a wicket with every ball I send down, just as I assume all good batsmen expect that in every ball there is a run for them. That's the way I look at bowling, as should any other 'quickie'. You've got to be positive like that, or bowling can become a lost cause. You can fall into the trap of becoming too analytical about your bowling: statistics show that you take a wicket on the average every six or seven overs you bowl, so all you have to do is bowl and it will happen. That's fatal. It will lead to you relaxing on the job and bowling within yourself. There's nothing like a touch of youthful exuberance, a dash of childish expectancy that you're going to do something this very ball.

When you are young you are inclined to believe that playing cricket is a natural function, that it just happens and that you don't have to give it very much thought. But the sooner you realise that you have to put a lot more thought into it than you ever dreamt was necessary, the sooner you will stand the chance of improving to greatness. From a bowler's point of view, you've got to gain an inner knowledge of batsmen, of what makes them tick and where they have technical and mental weaknesses. It takes a conscious effort to listen and learn, to talk to those whom you think can increase your knowledge. Even though you are a bowler, you should make batsmanship your study so that you are better able to 'work out' a batsman who is settling in and giving you trouble. Take a look at Graham McKenzie. He has obviously lost the ability to blast out a *good* batsman with sheer pace, but just watch him work a batsman out. It's sheer joy to see him letting his experience flow out of his arms and legs and fingers as he goes to work on a batsman. Of course, Garth has been around for a long time and you'd expect him to be able to do this to perfection. But, acquire Garth's experience at a young age by learning at every turn and the world will be at your feet.

I look on each game, each ball as an individual challenge. It has to be thought out and carefully prepared. Before each ball I take a deep breath and throw everything into my run-up. Before each game I also take a deep breath and throw everything into getting myself mentally ready for the confrontation. You can't expect to arrive at the ground and plug into some dressing-room device that charges you up ready to take on the world. It doesn't happen that way, ever. I start working on myself days before a big game and by the time I arrive at the ground I'm usually raring to go. That's important for any sportsman, but especially so for a fast bowler who has to deliver the first blow of a game right on target and fast, so that he can take charge from the very start of proceedings. I can vividly recall how excited I used to get before a match with the local juniors. I'd get so keyed up with anticipation that I'd get blood noses the night before the game. Those blood noses are a fragment of my past, but I still enjoy the pleasant sensation of a slight jump in the pulse-rate every time my cricket ground for the day hoves in sight. I hope that feeling will never leave me.

The game has changed a lot in recent years and team approach has had to change with it. It might have been possible in the past to take a team onto a field knowing that if each individual did his best you should succeed in winning the match. Nowadays, though, you can't take that approach and you can be pretty certain that when a first-class team goes onto the field it has a collective strategy all planned out for that particular game. This is usually arrived at during a pre-match meeting of the whole team, normally the day before the match. This meeting is chaired by the captain and will consist of an analysis of each member of the opposing side. Their strengths and weaknesses are discussed and their recent performances dissected in considerable detail. For instance, WA might set out to attack Keith Stackpole by setting a wide fine leg and bowling a few bouncers at him early in his innings in the hope that Stacky's love for the hook may lead to his downfall through a miss-hit stroke to fine leg. But, if it became clear that

Stacky was either not going to hook or was playing the stroke so well that to bowl short to him was just offer him easy runs, it would be time for a change of plan. Then we would move into our alternative, which would be to pitch the ball well up just outside the off-stump and under no circumstances drop any short on the hook or cut. After a while, if we were lucky, Stacky would get fidgety and go for the drive that wasn't 'on', and it would be up to the men in the slips cordon to finish the job. It gave the captain and the bowler, not to mention the whole team, a great lift to see one of their plans come off. It brought us all together, we would *all* share in that dismissal in some way. But one had to be flexible. You may attack Doug Walters with great optimism with deliveries short of a length on or outside the off stump, but if he survived that initial onslaught you had to start thinking about containing the little fellow, because there just weren't any other chinks in his armour when he was batting well. But an astute captain like Invers would work away on a player and, fortified by hints that may have come out of the team meeting, try something different for a while before moving on to another approach.

In these meetings a good captain will take particular care of his younger players and bring them into the discussion as much as possible. He'll make sure that they follow the comments about opposing players, as at this stage in their career it's unlikely that they have acquired this detailed knowledge through experience. It's often said that there's no short cut to experience and in many ways this is true. But experience isn't just counted by the number of runs you've scored or the wickets you've taken or even the number of games you've played. It is basically the amount of time you take to learn. I've known players who have had all the experience in the world but haven't learnt a thing nor showed any signs of doing so. Learning and experience are very closely related and although in the final analysis you've got to go out and do it, a young player can save himself a great deal of frustration and heartbreak by absorbing this kind of information from older players.

One of the important side-effects of these meetings is that they go a long way to creating team spirit. There have been a lot of attempts to analyse team spirit and I don't think I am able to add anything to all the studies that have already appeared. But if I can't analyse it I can certainly recognise it and I have seen on many occasions the miraculous effect it can have. One of the problems that a good individual player has to face is that there comes a time when he has to submerge his own identity for the common good of the team. No team can work as eleven people, it can only function at its highest level as a unit of one. But making that happen is not an easy achievement. In fact, I wonder whether it is indeed possible to *make* it happen at all. It seems to be an almost magical quality which is either there or not. If it's not there everything feels 'flat' and nobody seems to care much about winning or losing, or about his teammates. The few occasions that I've played in teams that have lacked team spirit are times that I'd like to forget. There's no pleasure at all in being an individual in such a team, it defeats all the purposes of the word 'team'. But, the experience of actually feeling team spirit is one of the greatest elations I can imagine. It is not something that can be turned on and off like a light, it just grows on a gathering of people, brought on by each person having an extra special feeling for the others around him. It's a feeling that everybody is behind you, that they all feel that no matter what you do you are trying your very hardest, and you know that they are doing the same. Team spirit can do far more to lift a person or a team than any amount of razzamatazz that a football coach may throw at his men in a pre-match address.

When we were in England in 1972 the Australian side's team spirit was boosted through the togetherness we shared when we were travelling from town to town on team buses or coaches. This was a wonderful opportunity to turn the heat on, and if any of the players was feeling a bit down in the dumps we could soon sort him out by a bit of special attention on the bus. We would all sing songs together, taking it in turns to make up choruses to a given tune, and few rough jokes would come out. I'd strongly recommend this means of travel for Sheffield Shield sides, but distances are so great in Australia that anything but air travel is out of the question. The beauty of a bus is that you are cut off from the public, there are no inhibitions or prohibitions and you can really get to know each other on a journey of a few hours. That's vitally important for team feeling. How can you feel for somebody if you don't really know him?

We had a 'different' type of team gathering in the West Australian side on a couple of our Eastern States tours. They were held in one of the hotel rooms from 7 o'clock to 8 o'clock on Sunday nights with an appointed Chairman, treasurer and two drink waiters. It would be the chairman's duty to convene the meeting, declare the rules of the meeting and the dress for the night. It would be the treasurer's job to record all the fines suggested by the members and ratified, after some humourous discussion, by the chairman. The drink waiters had the toughest task — to keep every glass filled or be fined rather heavily by popular vote!

When you are away from home and living out of hotel rooms and suitcases for long periods, it does present a problem for a Test captain to keep his team together and in the highest of spirits. There are all sorts of things which can waylay him, such as the ever-present possibility of factions developing, particularly built around the different States from which the party came from. There is also the age difference between the members of the party, often with

15 years separating the oldest and the youngest players. And, of course, there are the widely varying off-the-field interests of the players. Some like going to movies often, others can't stand that but don't mind going for a few drinks at a hotel. Some like golf, others don't play at all. Then there are those players who become easily depressed because they are missing their wife and children and their home life. The captain of a team on tour, particularly one of the duration of an Australian tour of England, faces a monumental task in keeping all his players happy and united. I take my hat off to Ian Chappell for the way he worked things out in 1972.

One of the things he insisted on was that the players remained in the dressing-room for an hour or so after play each day. It's something widely practised in first-class cricket in Australia and it works wonders in building team feeling. Sometimes young players feel a bit left out of it, because they don't know the 'ropes', but they are encouraged to remain and join in, to the benefit of themselves and their team. The system is that the team which has been batting for most of the day grabs a few bottles of beer or cool drink and drifts into the opposing side's rooms about 10 minutes after stumps have been drawn. That 10 minutes gives players on both sides a chance to cool down and have their private post mortems on the day's play. When the 22 players are all in together the newcomers get a rare opportunity to rub shoulders with the champions of the day. It also gives players a chance to patch up any differences that there might have been out in the middle. I've seen fellows who have bitterly contested on the field during the day, smiling away together over a beer in the dressing-room when play's all over.

I was surprised and disappointed in England in 1972 to find that this get together isn't generally accepted by English cricketers. Still Ian Chappell made sure we didn't fall into their bad habits and one example of that stands out in my memory of that tour. It was during the Third Test at Trent Bridge and it was the end of a day in which we had made big inroads into the English first innings. We had all had a pretty hard day in the field, particularly the bowlers, and we settled down into what chairs were available in our dressing-room and prepared to unwind over a couple of pints with the opposition. Only about four England players bothered to come into our rooms — and they stayed for only half an hour. Then it was just the Aussies. The team spirit was so high that come 9 o'clock, two-and-a-half hours after stumps, Bob Massie, Dave Colley and I were still sitting on the players' balcony, singing merrily (if you could call it singing!) and watching the groundsmen below us finishing their work in the fading light.

I think team spirit must come down from the captain. For if he doesn't have any feeling for his men, there's no way they can have feeling for him or their teammates. At the start of the England tour Ian Chappell made a big effort to bring the younger and less-experienced members of the party into the limelight. He treated every member of his team as though they were all champions.

John Inverarity, captain of the West Australian side, was similarly thorough in his approach to building confidence in his players and spirit in his team. He is an extremely hard worker at his game, and that has always been a wonderful example to an up-and-coming player. Invers is very courageous. His career has been dotted with injury and he has always battled on without letting us know how much he is suffering. It's only later that you realise just how much pain he has endured to lead his team onto the field. This sort of action gains far more respect and admiration of the men than a thousand hollow words. Invers gives so generously and unselfishly of his time and energy to his men. He will spend hours working with one man on his technique or his confidence. He will boost you when you need it, 'roast' you when you need it, advise you when you need it and ask questions that stimulate you to think more about your game. But above all he gives everything to his team — and they just can't do anything but give their all in return. One thing he has taught us is to want success desperately for ourselves and for our team, but most of all we must really *want* each of our teammates to succeed. He wants us to reach a situation where we feel just as pleased if one of our mates scores a century or takes a bag of wickets as if we had done it ourselves. And I think that when eleven men achieve this elevated feeling, then they've got team spirit.

8

Somebody once asked me what was the most important thing cricket had given me. It was a difficult question, because although the obvious answers, like the great pleasure in doing something well or the fact that it has opened a lot of doors for me, are true, neither of these are the most important for me. The most important in my case is the unique chance to travel, and the opportunity to meet people and make good friends. Cricket, perhaps more than any other sport I can imagine, gives you the chance to make lasting friendships. When you are away on tour with a bunch of lads there are so many opportunities to get to know them, so many times when relationships can be developed. Take the longest of tours, the five months or so in England when you share a room with the same player for so many weeks, when you ride in the same bus and go to so many of the same places with all your teammates. What a wonderful experience it is for a young man to take his first look at the world in such circumstances.

I was really lucky in 1972 because I had a great room-mate in David Colley and we had an excellent captain in Ian Chappell, who made a big effort to ensure that his men stuck together and that team morale and feeling never sagged. When you contemplate it, the captain of such a touring side faces an enormous task in keeping his team as a unit. His youngest player may be 18 and his oldest 35, so there is an immediate age difference which takes some breaking down. Then there is a tendency for players to polarise into their different States and the captain has to fight against factioning. Ian went out of his way early in the 1972 tour to speak to us all on our own and let us know what he was trying to do and what he expected of us individually. That personal touch, and many other examples of that nature, made him the successful captain that he was on that tour. The captain has all sorts of pressures on him, such as the responsibility for his team's performance and its image off the field.

In England he and the manager are the only people allowed to speak to the press and he gets a fair number of curly ones thrown at him by the highly-competitive Fleet Street team that follows the side around. He had to contend with the sort of blow-ups in the press that comes when an army of men can't interview players but are expected to get stories. Writers often have to grasp at straws and create stories which are usually blown up out of all proportion to the truth. Take the 'sunbaking at Lord's' incident. It was a warm day during the Second Test match and some of our lads took the opportunity to strip off to the waist and grab a bit of sun out on the players' balcony. We would have been clearly visible to some sections of the members' stand and people could have seen us from way over the other side of the ground, but what did that matter? The press got stuck right into us, claiming that we were nothing but larrikins, but after all you can see the top half of a man's body on any summer's day on the beach. Perhaps it was more than significant that in that particular game we were giving the Englishmen a right good hiding, and that the particular section of the members' stand near our rooms was struck silent on more than one occasion as Bob Massie raced through the front line of the English batting. I was on the field at the time, but I was told that our non-playing team-mates in the side wasted no time or energy in reminding those dumbstruck MCC members that they should be applauding Bob's brilliant bowling. I don't think that went down too well!

Another area where the press got stuck into us was what they called 'mouthing-off' on the field. In the games I played against the counties there was the odd word said between the players, but no more than would be said in a Saturday afternoon grade game in Perth, or a Sheffield Shield match. I think a little bit of needle, as long as long as it's not taken too far, adds a bit of flavour to a game and brings the best out of good players. A lot of things said on a cricket field are simply players giving vent to their own frustrations and are more than likely aimed at themselves, but can be wrongly taken as an insult by another player.

I sometimes wonder where these writers get their information: they certainly can't get a balanced report as the Australian players aren't allowed to be interviewed. Some of it is harmless, though, as in the case when Ian Chappell, Graeme Watson and I were 'signed up' for a game with a pub side down in Sussex. We had been to Robertsbridge to do some business and called into one of the local pubs to have a drink on our way home. The fellow behind the bar must have recognised us because he asked us if we would put our names on a blackboard in the bar for a game against another pub in the town. Somehow the story got back to

London and the next day it was in print, together with a picture of our signatures.

During the tour of England there were many long periods spent in the dressing-room with little to do as rain drizzled down outside and outlook for play diminished as each dreary hour passed away. This situation is tailor-made for tour comedians to take the stage and help pass the time. I already had a fair idea what a funny fellow Bob Massie is, but it was a real eye-opener for the other members of the touring party when Bob got started. He is about as dry as the Sahara Desert, and when he's telling a story you could be excused for thinking he's a preacher giving a rather dull sermon, until it dawns on you that he's actually taking the 'mickey' out of somebody, and it might be you! Bob's speciality is mimicking famous, and not-so-famous, people. In this sphere he is almost without peer in my experience. In fact the word got around London so much about his imitations of commentator John Arlott that curiosity got the better of Arlott himself. In the end he asked Bob around to his home for dinner for a private 'viewing'. The story is that John was so impressed by Bob's version of Arlott calling a day's play that he even gave him a bit of coaching in the West Country burr to smooth off a few of the rough edges. Bob is also absolutely brilliant at copying the actions of bowlers from all the sides we have come up against, and the foibles of batsmen don't escape his notice, either. During his period of coming and going between Australia and professional engagements in Scotland Bob worked for a while as an assistant groundsman at the WACA Ground in Perth, and I suspect that rather than devoting all his time to painting benches and driving lawnmowers, Bob was perfecting his imitations. At the end of it he was able to give a flawless imitation of the groundsman, little Roy Abbott, in action.

These dressing-room funny men can be worth their weight in gold for a captain, because when you're away from home for long periods all sorts of things can combine to bring down your spirits. It might be the weather, your form or just plain boredom. There's not much boredom when Ashley Mallet is around. He is a very funny man, not just because he can tell jokes or humourous stories better than anybody else, but because he can actually cause them! Ash is one of the clumsiest people I've ever seen. He can trip over, knock things over, spill his drinks and forget things better than any man I know. He is a great advocate and disciple of an Australian-born (I think) cult called the Limp-Fallers. Their particular performance is to fall from the upright to the horizontal in any bizarre manner and with as much colour as possible without doing themselves any damage. The great West Australian cartoonist Paul Rigby, now living and working in London, was one of the fore-runners of this cult, which has since manifested itself in pubs and dance-halls and private parties all over the world. It reached a pinnacle of publicity when Riggers was asked to appear on a television show in England compered by another West Australian, Rolf Harris, to explain and demonstrate the art of limp-falling. Riggers did this brilliantly and explained to the world the physical and philosophical sides of the practice. It is my earnest belief, however, that there's nothing philosophical about limp-falling as far as Ashley Mallett is concerned. Classifying himself as a limp-faller is his way of explaining the reason for his past, present and future acts of clumsiness. In other words, I reckon that limp-falling comes naturally to Ash. The only thing is that when he does it on purpose he usually caüses himself more damage than when he does it naturally! Like the time he was cajoled into a limp-fall at a team function on the eve of our departure from England in 1972. We were all pretty 'high' on the thoughts that the tour was over and that we were soon to be back home again. Doug Walters and Ross Edwards sat next to Ash and for some time pleaded with him to give the proceedings a lift by doing one of his limp falls. Finally, and suddenly, he gave in and, with only a quick look over his shoulder to see if all was clear, flung himself backwards out of his chair in the limp fall to end all limp falls. The only trouble was that Ash had misjudged the distance between his chair and the wall behind him and the result was a far-from-harmless fall. In fact, several doses of alcohol were needed to restore his composure!

I can think of few more cosy scenes than a happy dressing-room. You can actually feel the warmth from your teammates, and it's even stronger than ever if one of the boys is a bit down and out, perhaps after a disappointing day in the field, a dropped catch that could have cost the match or a poor performance out in the centre with the bat. That's when your comrades can be at their best. That's when the warm atmosphere can rebuild your confidence in yourself and in your side.

The dressing-room has always been, and I suppose always will be, the birth-place for nicknames and how Australians love to give each other nicknames! In the rooms, perhaps while your side is batting, there is plenty of time to settle down to the trial and error of finding a nickname that fits. Some are better than others, some last for a while and are then updated, but some are pearls and remain for ever. For example, the New South Wales and Australian spinner Johnny Gleeson was a bit of a mystery man when he was on tour with the Australian second team in New Zealand early in his career and he picked up a nickname there which he is sure to carry to his grave. It is CHO, springing from the three words Cricket Hours Only, meaning that it was during cricket hours only that his teammates knew where he was. Another clever one was pinned on Queensland wicket-keeper John Maclean, also after a second team tour to New Zealand. John had the habit of plastering white cream over his face to protect it from the sun, so much so that he often looked like a ghost. In a steal from the Phantom comic strip the boys dubbed him Ogo, 'Oh Ghost who walks.' Another Queenslander, batsman Phil Carlson who played the 1973 season for Bacup in the Lancashire League, came onto the scene just as the book *Portnoy's Complaint* appeared. His initials, and that of the book, being P.C., Carlson picked up the nickname of Portnoy. New South Wales batsman Alan Turner was dubbed Fitterun, a play on the trade of fitter and turner. Among the others are Greg Chappell (Local, because of the similarity of his frizzy hair to that of the locals in the West Indies); Ashley Mallett (Rowdy, because he hardly says 'boo' all day); Max Walker (Tangle, because of his awkward and tangle-footed bowling action); Paul Sheahan (Timbers, many years ago); Keith Stackpole (Humphrey, because of resemblance to Humphrey Bear); Bob Massie (Fergie, because of his Scots leanings and the well-known brand of tractors called Massey-Ferguson); Bruce Francis (Mule, because of the movie character called Francis, the talking mule); and Ross Edwards (Taj, because he was long known only as Rossi and along came a top-line Australian racehorse called Taj Rossi. That one was helped along by the fact that he had visited the Taj Mahal and is fascinated by India and Indians).

Where did I get FOT? Well it's a long story and it goes back to my very early days in first-class cricket for Western Australia. Tony Lock was then captain of the State side and I'm sure nobody aggravated him more than I did in those days. I was pretty scatter-brained and not quite 'with it' most of the time. I guess you could say I was very green and a little overawed. Locky used to bury me in the field at fine leg and third man whenever he could and he used to despair that I would ever keep up with the game sufficiently to change my position when the batsman on strike changed. He was, I am forced to admit, forever having to check to make sure I had remembered to move. It was a constant source of annoyance to him and the crunch came one day when there was a lefthander partnering a righthand batsman in a Sheffield Shield game at the WACA Ground. Locky used to call me 'Lil' in those days and after screaming out 'Lil' to me a dozen times to remind me that I should be fine leg (for the righthander) rather than third man (for the lefthander) he finally flipped his lid. He shouted, loud enough for the whole city of Perth to have heard, 'Come on Lil, you're like a Flippin' Old Tart.' John Inverarity, then vice-captain of the side, had worked hard to find a good nickname for me. He had started off with 'Falcon' because my nose, chin and sideburns had given me something of a falcon-like profile. Then he tried 'Water' and 'Tiger' after different types of lilies, but Invers wasn't happy with any of them. Like a flash he leapt upon Locky's derisive shout and I was christened FOT . . . Flippin' Old Tart! It's a constant reminder of Locky and of my youth.

But you have to have a go yourself every now and then. One of the things that griped me about the tour of England was the number of official functions we had to attend as a team. I think it would have been a far better idea to throw them all together and have one big wing-ding get-together with everybody and get it over in one hit. At one particular function latish in the tour, when my patience was almost at its limit, I was talking to a rather well-to-do gentleman who was doing his best to promote the conversation. This gentleman asked me what my father did for a living. 'He's a turf scientist,' I replied rather matter-of-factly. At that the gentleman pricked his ears up noticeably and I could tell he was dying to ask me just what a 'turf scientist' was. Curiosity finally got the better of him and he said, rather formally, 'That sounds interesting, what does that entail?' You should have seen the look on his face when I told him that Dad was a lawnmower man!

Much as I loved England, the thrill of playing an Ashes

series there and the pleasure of meeting some wonderful people, I believe that tour was far too long. The emphasis is more and more on the Ashes, and in that light the string of matches against the Counties, Scotland, the Minor Counties and the Combined Universities could have been pruned back to possibly half a dozen games outside the Tests and the mini-Tests. We even endured the ridiculous situation in 1972 of playing one county twice. Counties could qualify for a game against the Australian touring team on the basis of the League table the previous season. This would not only reduce the pressure on the touring team but would also add considerable interest to the County games during that season.

There are all sorts of fringe benefits in having a short tour. The players benefit by not having to be away from their families and jobs for so long and there would be financial benefits if things were properly organised. For instance, the cumbersome touring party of 17 players, a manager, assistant-manager, secretary, scorer-baggageman and physiotherapist could be pruned back. Instead of being away for almost five months, a tour of five Tests, three mini-Tests and a handful of county games could well be over in two months and could be capably handled by 14 players, a manager and help hired locally in the form of a scorer and physiotherapist. The difference in the costs would be enormous with the wages, fares and accommodation for five or six people eliminated and the tour cut to half its present duration. And there would probably be the same income from the tour, because I doubt very much if any money is made from the extra games that are played between Australia and the counties. Of course, the condensed nature of the tour would put greater pressure on the 14 players involved, but because of the extra profit these players could perhaps be well paid for their efforts over the two months. One of the problems with these long tours is that they occupy the whole of the southern winter. By the time you get back to Australia there's no time to take a breather and rest up for the new season at home. A shortened tour would give the players a chance to have a couple of months break and cut down the risk of going stale. I am sure that was one of the problems Bob Massie faced at the end of the 1972 tour and which contributed to his fading out of the Australian scene. I faced it myself and it's not easy to overcome. You could also pick your touring months, say June and July, which are likely to have the best weather and which include school holidays to help boost the gates.

A couple of matters arise each time Australian sides go on tour to England which grate a bit on the players. These are the agreement we have to sign concerning press interviews, and the restrictions on returning to play in England after the tour. Players are barred from making statements to the press and I think this is a pretty poor state of affairs. On the one hand you are considered good enough to represent your country abroad and on the other you are thought not mature or capable enough to be interviewed by a journalist. At times this is the same as depriving a player of the ability to earn money, because, particularly in England, there is good money to be made by sportsmen for stories in the big papers. Obviously the Board is trying to protect the unsuspecting young players from ruthless reporters, but surely a touring party executive could sit in on any interview or peruse the story before it is printed. Older and more experienced players should be able to look after themselves.

The other restriction on England tourists is that they must not return to play in that country within two years of making a tour with an Australian side. Again I think the Board is taking liberties with the players' rights, stopping them earning money and advancing in the game. I gather this rule is aimed at keeping our best players at their best to play for Australia, but the player *must* retain his right to go where he wants in the cricket world.

On a quick calculation I'd say I've been lucky enough to have played on about 100 cricket grounds in Australia, England, New Zealand and the West Indies. Each one has its own charm, its own characteristics and its own appeal. The range starts at the bottom with some of the 'grounds' I've come across in West Australia's more remote country areas. On my first tour with the WA side I just drank in everything about the four State association grounds we played on. I love the atmosphere of the Sydney Cricket Ground with its beautiful green-turretted grandstands and its unique Hill, the mausoleum that is the Melbourne Cricket Ground, the tropical atmosphere of the Brisbane Cricket Ground and the beautiful 180-degree vista from the players' balcony in the members' stand at the Adelaide Oval, dominated by the cathedral on the left and the Adelaide hills in the hazy distance. But it took a tour to England to take me to what must be the top of the scale as far as grounds are concerned. Lord's.

This cricketing Mecca has earned its title as the world's No. 1 arena for the game. Back in the days when dreams were almost realities I often strode the grass of Lord's as I listened to descriptions of Test matches there. I had all sorts of pre-conceptions about Lord's and it was my highest ideal in cricket to play on its hallowed turf. I am glad to say that I wasn't in any way deflated when I first 'strode boldly upon the grass of Lord's'. It was fabulous. You could almost 'touch' the atmosphere and the echoes of the Lord's tradition were almost loud enough to hear. The ground setting is so appealing, too. Everywhere is the very character of cricket. My heart was pounding with pride the first time I walked down the players' race onto the ground, past all the gentlemen of Lord's, all done up in their Sunday best, the yellow and red of the MCC tie prominent and an air of expectancy on their mildly-curious faces. Here were some of the really knowledgeable men of the game and out in the middle you could almost hear them making comparisons with the greats of the past. Indeed, if you closed your eyes for a moment you could easily conjure up a picture of some of the past champions who have spiked that turf. The playing surface is like a dream, with the immaculate finish of a billiard table. No matter where you are in the field you feel that the crowd is right there next to you, eyes glued to the action, whether it's fast or slow, dull or jam-packed with interest. It's hard to imagine this of the dyed-in-the-wool English supporter, but I sensed that the gentlemen of Lord's were 'with' me even though I played for the opposition.

Cricketers in a bunch love doing one thing more than anything else: talking cricket! On long aeroplane flights there is time to kill and it isn't long after take-off before small groups have formed to have a thrash about 'the game'. Of course, if you've been away for a couple of months there comes a time when even that subject gets a bit thin!

It was on a long flight home from our 1973 tour of the West Indies that talk died out and I whiled away an hour or so by picking the team of the 12 best men I've played with or against. It was a fascinating study, seeking the perfect blend, and it was great fun sifting through all the players I've come across since that day in 1969 when it all began for me. I came up with a team that I reckon would toss a similarly-chosen team from any decade.

In batting order, I started with Barry Richards and Bill Lawry; Richards the personification of batting perfection and Lawry the lefthanded grafter who was so reliable. I had to gloss over the like of Boycott, Edrich and Fredericks.

Ian Chappell was No. 3 and captain of the side. He is so adaptable, he can play a dogged role when the side is in trouble, or he can pile on the agony after a good opening. He played one of the greatest innings I've seen on a treacherous turner at Port of Spain, Trinidad, in the second innings of the Third Test in 1973.

The No. 4 slot went to his brilliant brother, Greg, so technically sound, such a graceful strokeplayer, the complete batsman. Greg is a superb all-round fieldsman as well as a useful seam bowler.

Who better than Doug Walters at No. 5? Despite his patchy tour of England in 1972, when he was having trouble with his technique, I still rate Doug as one of the soundest and most comprehensive batsmen I've seen. You very rarely see Walters struggle. Either he gets 'em well or he doesn't get any! He's also a very handy medium-pace bowler and brilliant cover fieldsman.

At the age of 38 Rohan Kanhai still batted at an average of 51.14 in the series against Australia in the West Indies in 1973. He was my No. 6. In younger days Kanhai was one of the most flamboyant strokeplayers the game has produced.

Then Gary Sobers. What a No. 7! He's a true all-rounder, a great batsman, a great bowler (fast, orthodox or wrist spin) and a great fieldsman. His sheer class nudged out Tony Greig to 12th man.

Wicketkeeper is Rod Marsh, by a whisker from Alan Knott. I rate the two together with the gloves but would rather have Rod's penetrating batting.

John Snow and Graham McKenzie for the new-ball attack. I place Snow out in front of all the quickies I've played with or against. Temperament, the ability to place the ball with precision, to make it cut off the wicket in England and lift sharply in Australia made him the champion that he was. That left the spinner's berth and what a difficult decision that was! Mallett, Gibbs or Lock? Mallett the up-and-comer, Gibbs the best 'offie' I've seen and Lock the master. I went for Lock, who has proved his ability in all conditions. His outstanding achievements in Australia, after a brilliant career in England, demonstrate his greatness.

The team, in batting order, was:

Barry Richards (South Africa)
Bill Lawry (Australia)
Ian Chappell (Australia)
Greg Chappell (Australia)
Doug Walters (Australia)
Rohan Kanhai (West Indies)
Gary Sobers (West Indies)
Rod Marsh (Australia)
John Snow (England)
Graham McKenzie (Australia)
Tony Lock (England)
Tony Greig (England) 12th man

9

If Helen hadn't been working whilst I was touring England with Ian Chappell's team in 1972 she and I could have ended up in serious financial difficulty. My pay whilst I was away was $20 a day plus a meal allowance which never covered the meals I needed to keep myself in trim for the rigours of such a long and arduous tour. That money on its own probably would have seen the two of us through and covered our commitments, like paying off the house, but only because no tax was taken off before I received my pay from the tour treasurer. As it was I was left with a serious tax problem because of my cricket earnings, meagre though they were during the 1971-2 and 1972-3 seasons. Helen and I had needed every penny of the money I received to live on and hadn't been able to put enough aside to pay our tax bill. Then we were hit with provisional tax as well and had to borrow money to pay that. During that tour of

England there were members of the party who were reluctant to buy themselves a decent meal because they just couldn't afford to spend the money. Australia's Paul Sheahan and Pakistani Majid Khan have made it quite clear what they think about virtually paying to play Test cricket. Sheahan hinted that this was one of the main reasons why he had phased out of playing for his country overseas, and Khan also looked closely at money matters when he told Pakistani officials that he would rather play for English county side Glamorgan than for his country because he would be far better off financially.

Khan's stand may have aroused the ire of the cricket purists but it did underline what has become a growing problem within the game. Things are looking up as sponsors are injecting an appreciable amount of money into the game, but there still is a long long way to go before cricketers are well paid in comparison with other professional or semi-professional sportsmen throughout the world. Money is not only important to get you by during your playing years, but is vital to put you on a good footing for the later years when you have to pick up the strings of employment on a serious basis for the first time. Employers who clamour for the services of top-line sportsmen have the habit of losing interest once their playing days are over and the glitter begins to tarnish. The job scrapheap is littered with men who placed sport first during their starry-eyed youth, and later regretted it.

There can be few better comparisons of what sport can mean to individuals in money terms than the one between the two Marsh brothers, Rod and Graham. Both are champions in their own spheres. Rod stands in a rare bunch of exciting international cricketers and his brother is in the top bracket of the world's golfers. Rod has great ability and above all enormous spectator appeal, but until recently he has been virtually giving his talents away without charge. Rod used to be a schoolteacher and in order to play cricket for WA and Australia he often had all sorts of complications with his job. He even went away on some tours on a leave-without-pay basis, and the cricket money he received just didn't go far enough. Of course there were times when his 'lost' days fell during school vacations when he was drawing his pay as well as his cricket money, and then Rod stood to make a few bob. Two factors have improved the situation for him. He has changed jobs and is now a sales promotion executive with an Australia wide building company. They could see the value of having an international sportsman on their staff and were able to reach a far more amicable agreement with Rod concerning his periods of absence from the office. That job was lined up for him by Ken Ferguson and Dennis Tobin, both great friends of mine and stalwarts of the Perth Cricket Club, who also later helped me to get a job with a national travel firm. Both Rod and I are payed a set salary for each twelve months, regardless of how many days we miss through cricket commitments. The second booster to Rod Marsh's income has been the gradual increase in the amount of sponsorship for cricket, which helps to keep his head above water. But where does it leave him in comparison with his celebrated brother? I'm no expert on golf, but I reckon Graham Marsh is in the top dozen golfers in the world, and that means his income could well be more than $100,000 a year. There is just no comparison in the amount of money Rod and Graham get from sport, even taking into account that Graham is a full-time professional. I know Rod is so often away from home that his wife, Ros, quite often gets the impression that her husband is a full-time cricketer! You can't justify the difference by saying that Rod plays some obscure sport. It just doesn't tally.

But the discrepancies don't end there. Take the example

of Chris Evert, the child prodigy tennis star who was reported to have earned more than $200,000 from her first year in the big-time. Indeed, throughout the American sporting network there must be thousands who earn far more than the average Australian Test cricketer. There are hundreds of soccer stars throughout the world who would look upon a Test cricketer's earnings as no more than pocket money. Closer to home, and this really hurts me, is the fact that there are probably a couple of dozen club footballers in WA who are paid about as much for their sport as Rod Marsh gets. And Australian Rules football isn't even played outside Australia!

It really is no wonder that the best of Australia's cricketers don't last much over the 30 mark. There have been many like Richie Benaud, Bob Simpson and Alan Davidson who called it a day when perhaps they had five more good years in them and I venture to suggest that it may have been partly because of the money problem within cricket. On the average English players last five to 10 years longer in the game than Australians. But they are more harnessed to the system because it is a business to them. They are full-time cricketers and they hang on and on, eking out a contract as long as they can. In their latter years they will move on to another club or to one of the Leagues just to keep going. 'Job' is a strange word to most of them and it is not uncommon for a county cricketer to 'go on the dole' because he can't get employment in the winter months. Of course, sponsorship is bringing in large sums of money for English cricket and no doubt players are improving their lot as a result.

Just how much do Australian cricketers earn? I've told you the terms of the 1972 tour, which far from lined the pockets of the 17 players who went in quest of the Ashes on that occasion. I must be fair and say that almost to a man we were happy to accept those terms before we left on that tour. And I must point out that we did enjoy some fringe benefits while on the tour, such as being able to buy things at the 'right price' wherever we went and occasionally receiving gifts to take home.

Pay scales are a little better when you play a Test match in Australia. I earned about $250 a Test in Australia, which sounds quite attractive at first, but which boils down to little more than an average week's wages after you deduct your expenses and 'lost' pay and then spread it over the nine days that you are away from home.

Pay for playing at interstate level is a joke. The WA Cricket Association jumped its pay to $11 a day for the 1973-74 season and when you work out that the Sheffield Shield season consists of eight four-day games you can see just how little that means. The player who loses his pay or his annual leave to make himself available for WA is well out of pocket. Again, sponsors are livening things up for cricketers in Australia and gradually pay scales are improving. But in the light of these figures it was no wonder that Greg Chappell had no hesitation in accepting an offer reported to be in the vicinity of $50,000 to leave South Australia and play for Queensland in the 1973-74 season. I believe that's the sort of money a player of Greg's calibre deserves. Perhaps the Queensland move is something of a precedent and players like Rod Marsh can hope for similar inducements to change their State allegiances.

I may be in danger of giving the idea that cricketers in Australia are little more than a bunch of money-grubbers, looking for a hand-out at every turn. That is far from the intention. Cricketers entertain a huge audience every summer, and if you think the Sheffield Shield crowds don't back up that statement just think of the number of calls received by the Sports Results Service when there is a cricket match in progress. And the cricket audience is becoming even bigger as a result of the lengthened and widened television coverage in Australia. In the light of all the pleasure they bring so many people, and bearing in mind the fact that an Australian first-class player's season starts with training in June and ends in April, I believe cricketers are grossly underpaid.

It is up to cricket's officialdom to realise this and do something about it. But immediately the subject arises, the issue becomes strangely clouded. Suddenly men lose their sense of values. During the day they see the need for realism as far as money in business is concerned, but at night around the cricket association meeting table they seem to suffer some sort of paralysis. It is a delusion that cricketers are prepared to go on 'paying' so much to play on the higher levels. We are moving with the times and unless cricket administrators are prepared to change, I can see a rift forming between the two which can only lead to dissatisfaction and, sooner or later, confrontation. Despite what sports administrators may say to the contrary, a game of any sort is only as good as the players taking part. Cricket administrators must realise this and start doing something about putting money matters straight.

I have often thought that all too many Australian cricket administrators at all levels are too interested in pushing their own barrow. They are too concerned about personal kudos to realise where the roots of the game lie: in the players of all ages. Some of them don't seem to bother two hoots about the players. They hide behind the committee-room doors and are often so removed from the playing side of the game that it's no wonder they are violently against change. Their 'it didn't happen in my day' attitude is one of the main causes of the stifling of progress in the sport today.

Of course, it would be unfair to leave it at that. There are many officials whose heart is in the right place and who give their time freely. Some of them step down a couple of rungs to reach the players and try to understand their problems. They have a compassion for the needs of the players and, fortunately for the prosperity of cricket in Australia, are far-sighted enough to realise the importance of moving with the times. I hope these men, whom I consider to be in the minority in our administrative set-up, will rise up and stand tall enough to sway the traditionalists in the future. Cricket needs them. It needs them to sweep through its networks and made something workable out of the often top-heavy structures that are weighing the game down.

It will take a long time for changes like that, but what of the immediate future? I firmly believe that cricket must move out of the era of traditionalism and the 'old school tie' and move into present-day get-up-and-go thinking. The game must be promoted and sold to the public and to prospective sponsors, for its own good and the good of the players. Why not pay top money for a promotions man with zeal, energy and ideas and let him package the game, and its players and sell the whole deal to the highest bidder? There's big money out there, not only potentially for the turnstile cash boxes, but in big business too, and cricket should be getting its share. Every week I read of enormous stake money for big-time horse races, golf tournaments, tennis titles, where cigarette companies, motor car manufacturers, mining companies and others pour money into 'superstar' events. Events like the Wills Masters in golf, the Sheraton Stakes in racing and the Benson and Hedges Cup in trotting. Naming major sporting events after sponsors goes on throughout the world and we have it in Australian cricket with the Gillette Cup knockout competition. That's great, but why not the X-brand Sheffield Shield and the Y-brand Test series between Australia and England?

I have often wondered if cricket administrators have

been reticent about attracting promoters to provide good money for the players because they are concerned about their ability to carry it on if the sponsor drops out. I know of one vigorous attempt to set up a players' fund in WA that reached an advanced stage and finally foundered, partly because of a lack of initiative from the WA Cricket Association. The idea was to bring in incentive money for our players from the business sector, in return for endorsements or even just for the love of the game. There was an alternative plan, by the same group of people, to aim for a really big figure, say $100,000, to set up a trust fund and to devote the proceeds from its investment as a perpetual return for the WA players. I don't know just how many of WA's top officials were aware of this plan, but those who were gave little encouragement and finally the idea died, despite a warm response by Perth businessmen. I believe this is the sort of thing the association should be actively working at, rather than snuffing it out. After WA won the Sheffield Shield in 1971-2 and 1972-3 the best the Association did for us was to turn on a meal for the players and their wives or girl-friends at a suburban hotel. A provident fund scheme, of a modest nature, *has* been initiated by the WA Cricket Association and perhaps that will grow to significant proportions over the years.

Should cricketers do something positive to improve their lot? Generally speaking, we are in the hands of the administration. They make up our minds for us, paying us what they think we deserve, offering us their terms and no questions asked. But 1974 was a significant one for players, because the Australian Cricket Board sought their opinions on certain matters and heard them personally from Ian Chappell after he had consulted each State captain. Maybe same good will come from that and any future gestures by the hierarchy. If necessary I think the players should take the bull by the horns and become militant! They should approach the Board and put their case: Player A *lost* $1200 to play for his country this year, player B was $250 out of pocket through playing for his State and it's not good enough'. Players should let them know what they want, then start haggling for a price. Perhaps there is an argument for a player's union in Australian cricket, just as they have a professional soccer player's union in England and, more recently, for footballers in Victoria. A union would form a combined front for talks on matters such as pay, accommodation and conditions.

If the players aren't getting enough, and by now you'd have the opinion that I think they aren't, where is the money going? We are aware that large sums of money are forthcoming from overseas tours by Australian sides, particularly to England now that there is a guaranteed return before the team even leaves Australia. It is obvious that most Tests in Australia are money-spinners, so what happens to it? The Board and associations maintain that they are scraping the bottom of the barrel. If this is so, then it must be time for some form of streamlining of the game's administration, even if it means selling out to the government or to private enterprise. I can envisage cricket in Australia becoming some kind of private enterprise by the turn of the century. It has happened in America, where baseball and basketball teams are privately owned, so why not here? With a team being run as a business, there would be no doubt about the promotion of the sport. Some of the so-called superstars of other sports are little better at their game than the first-change bowler for Australia, yet who has ever heard of him? He simply hasn't been professionally promoted. I'm sure every international cricketer has a list of attributes which could be picked out and built on by a clever promotions man to make him more appealing to the public. It's something that is grossly neglected in our game. Indeed, those traditions I've been talking about run so deep that cricket administrators often react strongly to a player being in some way out of the ordinary. It appears their first thought is to do their utmost to knock that 'colour' out of him and bring him back to the traditional mould of a cricketer. They are blind to the fact that, even if he is a bit of a renegade, at least he's different and he's just what the public wants. Players like Allan 'Froggy' Thompson, of Victoria, and even Rod Marsh, in his early days, brought life to Australian cricket through their flamboyant character. But officialdom has moved to quell their natural flair and make them conform. Fortunately for cricket, neither has been brought to heel. And what a wonderful influence Colin Milburn had on the game in his all-too-short career at the top. He was something different and people really warmed to him.

I can see teams being privately-owned, run as a tight-knit business by men with the highest business qualifications. By the year 2000 I can see a new-look Sheffield Shield with, say, three teams each from New South Wales and Victoria, two each from Western Australia, South Australia and Queensland, and one from Tasmania. The population of Australia will be able to support 13 top-class teams, interstate travel will be easier and the games would be so professionally handled and promoted that they would compare favourably with the baseball competitions of North America today. With the power of such a super-league, owners of the teams in each State would pool together to establish their own ground for use by all teams for that State. There would be no room for rained-off matches, so synthetics would be widely used for the playing surfaces, durable, predictable and weathertight. There could be interchangeable wicket areas — a fast bowler's wicket for the first innings, a spinner's track for the second. The games would still be on a four-innings basis, but the two first innings would be played on one day, the second two on the next. Points would be scored at the end of each day and tallied up to give an overall winner. Certainly it would be 'manufactured' sport, but that has worked to great advantage with other sports in other countries and I can see no logical reason why it wouldn't work here. Life just won't stand still for cricket. It will have to step up its pace and be prepared to let its antiquated traditions go by the board if it is to have any appeal with the public in the 21st century.

10

Since I first played for the South Belmont juniors many years ago my attitude towards cricket has taken a couple of turns. At that stage I could think of only one thing: To become a Test player and be the world's best cricketer for ever. That was my dream and it was so compelling that it interfered with my school life, so that I couldn't concentrate on my work and finally couldn't wait to leave school and get on with my cricket. When I finally made the State team this only served to heighten my need to climb the final rungs on cricket's ladder.

Reaching the top was bliss, for a while. But I was married and I soon realised that touring around with cricket sides all the time wasn't all it was cracked up to be. I started missing Helen and during the long spell away from her in England in 1972 I decided this wasn't for me for much longer. It wasn't the hard work I had to put into staying at the top, it was simply that I didn't relish the thought of being away from Helen so often and for so long. At that stage I envisaged a short sweet career with a retirement from Test cricket at the age of 26 or 27. After that I could pick and choose my first-class and club cricket pursuits. It would be a matter of how I felt at the time. But I guess cricket was deeper in my blood than even I had imagined. When I spent the 1973-4 summer on the sidelines of Test and first-class cricket in Australia, taking a spell while my back knitted and regained strength, I realised just how much cricket meant to me. As I endured those months of sheer frustration I knew I wanted many more years at the top, if that was possible.

I know it's not going to be easy to regain the standards needed to win my place back at the head of the Australian attack. But I'm doing my utmost to ensure that nothing stands in my way to that goal. I have spent the winter months building up strength and stamina, visiting the University of WA's physical education department laboratory three times a week. There Dr Frank Pyke, a former first-grade cricketer with the Perth club, worked out a stiff programme of exercises for me which are aimed at strengthening every part of a fast bowler's physical make-up. These visits have been longer and harder than any other training routines I've ever taken on, but I have always been spurred on by the need to get to my best-ever fitness to ensure a successful comeback for WA and, hopefully, Australia. There has been emphasis in the exercises on building up my back to help take the load off my spine when I bowl at full speed. I am confident that the fractures have fully knitted and that I'll have no further trouble from my back. But no doctor can give me a guarantee of that and I guess I couldn't expect one.

I have that burning ambition I've spoken of, that never-say-die desire to succeed, but if I've done everything in my power and I fail I'm sure I'll be able to accept it. I'll be bitterly disappointed in myself if that is the case, but I'll find something else to occupy my time. Family life is so important to me that I'm sure I'll be around the house a lot more and there's nothing wrong with that. Helen is very tolerant of my cricket demands, but I'm sure she'd admit she wouldn't be too downhearted if I could spare more time at home.

But my programme doesn't really encompass failure at the first hurdle. It has been a very carefully-planned programme, right down to changing my job to ensure that work won't interfere too much with my cricket at this stage. After I returned from the West Indies in the winter of 1973 I bought a partnership in a contract cleaning business and left the bank. My partner and I worked extremely hard to get things going and were starting to see the rewards of our labours when I reached the cross roads. I badly wanted to make it again at cricket but working up to 13 hours a day every day didn't fit into the routine, so I had to make the agonising decision to quit my partnership and look for a more suitable job. It was tough having to pass up the wonderful business opportunity I had with the cleaning partnership, but the call of the cricket big-time was too strong.

My enforced break from first-class cricket has certainly given me newfound energy and enthusiasm for the game. It also gave me a valuable learning period as captain-coach of the Perth club. I feel that with all the training at the university too, I should be better-equipped for the 1974-5 season than for any other season I've played. I think I've learnt a valuable lesson from my experiences, and that is that you can't go on trying to bowl at a million miles an hour every ball, every over, every day. That used to be my theory about fast bowling, fire away as fast as you can, no matter what the conditions, no matter how fast or slow the wicket. I used to think you could beat a good batsman with pace through the air, even if the wicket was plumb slow. Now I appreciate that perhaps that ill-founded theory of mine probably caused my back injury and cost me a season in first-class cricket.

So now I am aware that the days of blasting 'em out are over. I have to approach the task from a different tack now, bowling most deliveries within myself and exploding only once or twice an over, just to let the batsman know who is the boss. I know I'll find it hard to resist the temptation to bowl flat out all the time, particularly if a batsman is settling in comfortably against me. But I know I'll be courting disaster if I try that, because I'll be leaving myself wide open to a recurrence of my back injury if I try to push on past the limits. But ever-present in my mind will be the consequences of another breakdown. The older I get the harder I'll find it to come back after an injury and of course there is always the possibility of permanent injury to my spine. I would certainly be upset if I thought I would never be able to play in England again. My goals include returning to England in 1975 for the world series and Tests against England. Then I'll set my sights on getting back there for the regular tour in 1977 and after that a lot will depend on my private and business life. But I have a strong yearning to play a couple of seasons of county cricket. I had a big offer from Derbyshire for 1973 and I was sorely tempted to follow that up further than I did. So if I'm still going strong and if my private and business life permits I'd like to be able to have a crack at county cricket, perhaps in 1978 and 1979. That's a long way off and who can tell what will happen between now and then?

Something else I'm looking forward to is the chance to do more work on radio and television. My break from first-class cricket in 1973-4 gave me a golden opportunity to get some experience in these fields.

During the 1972 tour of England I underwent a speed test in the nets at Lord's and organised by the BBC. An electronic device was set up to measure the speed of the delivery. There were a few hitches like the fact that I was bowling into a fair wind, I had to hit the stumps before a speed was recorded and I had the team manager, Ray Steele, breathing down my neck and reminding me not to wear myself out because we had a Test coming up in a couple of days. I was also operating off a shortened run, but still recorded a couple of deliveries over 80 miles per hour. A cricket enthusiast was also reported to have timed a delivery of mine in the international match against the Rest of the World in Melbourne in January, 1972, and recorded a reading above 90 miles per hour.

Will I ever achieve those speeds again? I am confident I will have the strength to do it. It will just be a matter of striking form again and I'll be right there.

It is such an exhilarating feeling to be able to make the ball fly off a good length and to make the world's best batsmen treat you with absolute respect because you are QUICK. I can barely wait.